Michigan Media Law

Second Edition

Benjamin Burns
Wayne State University

Dawn Phillips Hertz

The McGraw-Hill Companies, Inc.
Primis Custom Publishing

New York St. Louis San Francisco Auckland Bogotá
Caracas Lisbon London Madrid Mexico Milan Montreal
New Delhi Paris San Juan Singapore Sydney Tokyo Toronto

McGraw-Hill
A Division of The McGraw-Hill Companies

Michigan Media Law

McGraw-Hill's Primis Custom Series consists of products that are produced from camera-ready copy. Peer review, class testing, and accuracy are primarily the responsibility of the author(s).

7 8 9 0 QSR QSR 0 9 8 7

ISBN-13: 978-0-07-240139-4
ISBN-10: 0-07-240139-7

Custom Editor: Jan Scipio
Printer/Binder: Quebecor Printing Dubuque.

Contents

Disclaimer

This book represents the efforts of the authors to assist journalists and journalism students in Michigan in understanding how the laws apply to the profession. You should not consider any statement in the book carved in stone. Both authors recognize there are exceptions to any rule, no matter how carefully drawn. And court cases can change the interpretation of the laws on a daily basis. We also know that newspapers make mistakes every day and they print lies and untruths every day that are presented to them as facts by people with something to gain or lose. That is the nature of recording history as it happens on deadline. Hopefully some of the advice contained herein will prove useful to you. Remember your best defense is to be full, fair and accurate in the first place. You may still get sued, but it will make your attorney's job much easier. If you find errors of fact within this text call them to our attention and we will fix them in subsequent editions. As David Lawrence, now publisher of the Miami Herald and then publisher of the Detroit Free Press said, "The search for truth is an elusive pursuit." We wish you good hunting out there.

Dawn Phillips Hertz and Benjamin Burns
June 1998

Benjamin Burns is a thirty year veteran of the newspaper business and a former executive editor of The Detroit News. He now serves as the Director of Professional Studies in the Department of Communications at Wayne State University, Detroit Michigan

Dawn Phillips Hertz has served as General Counsel to the Michigan Press Association for 18 years. She represents many media clients in libel defense and access cases and answers media questions on the Michigan Press Association Hotline. Her offices are in Troy, Michigan.

Michigan Media Law, A Newsroom Guide

Preface

The First Amendment to the U.S. Constitution is the cornerstone of media law, 45 words which allow U.S. journalists to serve the public. It is mirrored by Article I, Section 5 of the Michigan Constitution.

The First Amendment states: "Congress shall make no law respecting an establishment of religion, or prohibiting the free exercise thereof; or abridging the freedom of speech or of the press; or the right of the people peaceably to assemble, and to petition the Government for a redress of Grievances."

Article I, Section 5 of the Michigan Constitution of 1963 states:"Every person may freely speak, write, express and publish his views on all subjects, being responsible for the abuse of such right; and no law shall be enacted to restrain or abridge the liberty of speech or of the press."

But neither the First Amendment nor the Michigan Constitution are an all-purpose shield.

The First Amendment does not say that journalists should treat politicians differently than private citizens; it does not say whether to name a rape victim. The First Amendment makes no mention of bias in coverage of the abortion issue or gay rights. And it offers no guidance on our responsibilities to our sources, according to Joann Byrd, former Washington Post ombudsman.

There is a general consensus to day that libel law in the United States is a system that doesn't work very well except for the lawyers. Barbara Dill in her column for Publishers' Auxiliary stated: "It costs too much, it takes too long, and clogs the courts with fencing matches that end most often in technical decisions that bypass the fundamental issues and satisfy neither side."

Allen Dershowitz, the celebrated attorney and Harvard law professor and frequently a figure of press coverage for his representation of celebrities like O. J. Simpson and Mia Farrow observed to the National Newspaper Association (NNA): "On the whole, I think, journalism is better than its ever been in history. The problem for journalists lies in their protection. The First Amendment . . . is a knife that cuts both ways. It gives you . . . protection, but it certainly doesn't guarantee excellence." "While no government body or official should be able to regulate journalism," he said, "if excellence is diminished to the point where the people's confidence in the media is shaken, then the First Amendment is also placed in danger." (as reported in Presstime, the NNA's magazine.)

The purpose of this manual is to help the news media achieve that requisite excellence by explaining Michigan media law in a clear and understandable fashion and advising you of the pitfalls and warning signals to help avoid court action while doing your job.

There can be a distinct chilling effect on a reporter when that phone call comes with an angry voice at the other end of the wire: "I'm going to sue you." It doesn't matter whether you are right or wrong no one likes the thought of the pain and agony of litigation. The reporter takes it as an attack on his or her integrity and credibility and fears it could damage a career, an editor knows that time and money spent defending against accusations in court is time and money not available to pursue gathering news for the paper, and a publisher recognizes that good legal help is expensive. Studies show how you react at that moment can either convince an aggrieved party to sue you or convince them that is not a good course.

This book is designed as a supplementary text for media law courses and as a practical guide for newsrooms so reporters, editors and publishers can answer most questions before a story gets into print and help you avoid that chilling moment of the libel threat and to know what to do when it occurs. It should also prove useful to government officials and attorneys who don't regularly practice media law. In newsrooms it should prove useful because it details some of the key cases that affect Michigan law and provides checklists to follow when you have questions. It also has forms to use when you are dealing with requests for information or orders from a judge to close a courtroom. It tells you what rights and privileges a reporter has in dealing with police agencies, the courts, private citizens and government. It tries to answer the questions you are likely to confront so reporters, editors and publishers can sleep a little easier at night.

It is our intent to update this volume periodically. If you have suggestions for cases that should be included or other information that should be added you can contact Dawn Phillips Hertz, Counsel for the Michigan Press Association at 827 N. Washington, Lansing, Michigan (517) 372-2424. Or contact Ben Burns, Professor, Department of Communication, Wayne State University, 193 Manoogian Hall, Detroit, MI 48202 or phone (313) 577-2627.

A considerable amount of the material used in this book has appeared in Michigan Press Association Bulletin articles written by Ms. Hertz. Other material has appeared in Michigan newspapers and magazines and in a variety of other publications and books on media law. We could not have completed the book without the assistance of some of Michigan's top corporate media legal advisors, who are listed in Appendix Six. We owe particular credit to Professor Jane Briggs-Bunting, Chair of the Journalism Department at

Oakland University, a practicing attorney, former Detroit Free Press reporter and author of "Legal Guidelines for Reporters in Michigan." That booklet, revised and updated in 1993 is available for $5 by contacting Ms. Bunting at PO Box 7, Oxford, MI 48371. We also acknowledge the excellent work "Florida Media Law", 2nd edition, by Professor Donna Lee Dickerson, at the University of South Florida in Tampa. Wayne State students did some of the research for this book on a grant by Wayne State University.

Any author proceeds from the sale of this book go to the Wayne State Journalism Institute for Minorities.

General Rules to Live By

1. **Get it right the first time.**

2. **Always be courteous.**

3. **Analyze statements about secondary persons who are named as carefully as you analyze the main figures.**

4. **Get the document.**

5. **In reporting on public officials focus on the connection between the subject matter and the public official's duties and qualifications.**

6. **In reporting on public <u>figures</u> focus your reporting to those issues that directly impact on that which makes them public figures.**

7. **Relatives of public officials and public figures are to be treated as private figures unless they have achieved public status in their own right.**

8. **Strive to be fair and balanced and recognize your obligation is to the reader, not the object of the story.**

9. **Words which imply criminal conduct should be used with care.**

10. **Sex is seldom safe.**

11. **Say it with gusto. Hyperbole means exaggeration. It's safer to safe say someone is "dumber than mud" rather than that person is "ignorant."**

12. **A rose by any other name may be libelous.**

13. **Reporters should leave opinions to the editorial page and the op ed page.**

14. **You are responsible for everything published in your media format whether someone else said it, even if it has quote marks, or is preceded by "alleged" or contained in advertisements. If you publish it, it is yours.**

15. **Always retain *(and maintain)* your sense of humor.**

Chapter 1

Check List for Libel

1. What portions of this article are contained in public documents?

2. Are any of the people identified (by name or description) in the article public officials?

3. Are any of the people identified (by name or description) in the article public figures? A. Full purpose?(rare); B. Limited? (common)

4. Is the article about a subject that is related to what makes this person a public official or figure?

5. Are all excerpts from public documents "fair and true reports" of the public documents?

6. Is the article balanced?

7. How many times have I tried to contact each individual identified in the article for comment or response?

8. Are all of the names spelled correctly?

9. Have I left out any relevant facts which might significantly change the story? If yes, why?

10. Do I have any doubts about the veracity of the story?

11. Have I published any facts about a person in the story that the person is trying to keep secret? If yes, are those facts newsworthy or merely titillating?

12. Are these facts "private" facts?

13. Did I identify each statement that might hurt the feelings or reputation of a person?

14. Has any person accused of a crime been arraigned before a judge?

15. Are there dangerous words such as fraud, bilk, forge, pilfer, lie, or cheat in the story?

16. Remember, truth is a defense for a libel action.

17. Hyperbole, epithets and insults are not ordinarily defamatory because they are not capable of conveying false facts.

Chapter 1

Libel Law in Michigan

By definition of the Michigan Supreme Court libel is:

1. **A false statement of fact.**
2. **Of and concerning the Complainant.**
3. **Which is defamatory i.e., lowers the person in the estimation of the community.**
4. **Published to third parties.**
5. **Unprivileged communication.**

The libelous statement must be made with fault amounting to at least negligence and the statement must be actionable.

But for the reporter or editor, the most important element to focus on in reviewing a story for the risk of libel is: **What is defamatory**?

In reviewing a story for the risk of liability for libel, the best approach is to review the story for all statements which you would be reluctant to make about your publisher's mother; that is to say that which is defamatory.

The term defamatory has nothing to do with truth or falsity. It has to do with statements that are derogatory, negative, likely to diminish reputation, likely to cause people not to associate with the individual. A defamatory statement about a subject is one that lowers the reputation of a subject in the community, that causes a lessening of the subject's esteem in the community, that causes people to disassociate themselves from the subject regardless of whether or not the statement is true or false.

For example, to say that Magic Johnson carries the HIV virus, is a defamatory statement: A true statement, but a defamatory statement. It affects his reputation. That statement will cause some people not to associate with him, on the basketball court and off. However, in terms of suing for damages, the truism is that "truth is a complete defense." Thus, the statement that Magic is HIV positive is a defamatory statement but not a libelous statement. He cannot sue for libel.

When reviewing a story, it is important to identify each statement that will tend to injure the reputation or the feelings of the subject about whom the statement is made. Looking for false statements does not work because reporters are not in the business of writing knowingly false statements. Thus, the best approach is to identify statements that are derogatory, unkind, nasty, defamatory. Once those statements are identified, then each statement can be analyzed to determine how the statement can be defended.

Is it true? Did it come from a government document? **(See Chapter 5)** Is the person a public figure or official? Do I have doubts about this statement? And, is it a government action?

The question, "Is this libelous?" should be the last question, not the first question.

The first question is "Is it defamatory?"

Some Statements Are Per Se Defamatory. That is to say, they are presumed to cause harm without proof of actual damage.

Criminal Conduct.

Any statement that someone has committed a crime is defamatory. Thus, any statement that someone has committed a crime should be carefully reviewed. Is there a government document such as a police report, or court file that will support the statement? Is there a qualified privilege that will attach to reports on this person such as the public official or public figure privilege.

Most newspapers in Michigan adhere to the rule that crimes are not reported until after the defendant is arraigned. As a practical matter, it is possible to print reports on crimes before the arraignment but only if a careful review is made of documents available, the circumstances and available defenses. But the fact that alleging criminal conduct is **per se** libelous, makes waiting for the arraignment the best rule to follow.

The **Rouch** case is a prime example of the risks of publishing before the arraignment. **(See Chapter 10 for a detailed discussion of this case.)** In this landmark Michigan libel decision, Mr. David Rouch was arrested and released on his own recognizance to await the prosecutor after the Christmas weekend. When the prosecutor reviewed the evidence against Mr. Rouch, he determined that there was insufficient information to issue a criminal complaint and dismissed the charges of the police. Although the newspaper was ultimately vindicated in a 10 year struggle as discussed elsewhere, if the newspaper had waited until a formal arraignment had occurred, it would not have reported on Mr. Rouch's arrest and would have avoided litigation.

Ordinary people make up the bulk of those charged with criminal conduct. Because they are not public figures or public officials, mistakes can be costly. There are limited privileges to protect reports of the press on private figures.

Therefore, the safest rule is to report criminal conduct only after an arraignment.

Words to Avoid.

Examples of words to avoid unless there has been an arraignment or a conviction, are:

> arson, theft, breaking and entering, bribery, embezzlement, assault, child abuse, murder, manslaughter, drunk driving, perjury, bad checks, and of course the grand daddy of them all, sexual misconduct.including words like rape, second degree criminal sexual conduct, and molestation.

Some of the most difficult words are those which have more than one meaning. They are words used in normal conversation to convey non criminal conduct as well as describing criminal conduct. The most notorious word in Michigan law is the word "charge". Again in the **Rouch v Enquirer & News of Battle Creek, 440 Mich 238; 487 NW2d 205 (1992),** the argument for 10 years in the courts was whether the statement that Rouch was **charged** with criminal sexual conduct was true or false because although the police had listed criminal sexual conduct as the reason for his arrest, the prosecutor had declined to bring formal charges on the resumption of business on December 26th.

In a painstaking opinion, Justice Boyle joined by four justices, ultimately held that the use of the word charged was not false; but it was defamatory.

The use of softer words, words that are not so punchy, can be as dangerous as their harder brethren. If you cannot defend the hard words, you cannot defend their softer version.

Thus, words which accuse or imply criminal conduct are defamatory per se. They must be used only when they can be *clearly* defended as outlined in subsequent chapters. Unless you have a government document to substantiate the charge or the individual is a public official or public figure and you have no doubts about the accuracy of the charge, do not include criminal accusations.

Moral Turpitude.

As the nomenclature suggests, this idea comes out of the past, but the danger is still with us.

Then there are the words which have been discontinued in the law but which nonetheless can have negative connotations:

> fraud, bilking, pilfering, cheating, lying, forgery. These words convey if not criminal conduct at least moral lapse. Other words to avoid are

words suggesting unfaithfulness to spouses, abuse of children, and abuse of animals.

Although these words can be used in non-criminal settings, it is wise to use less loaded words. State your facts and let the reader draw the conclusion rather than using short cut terminology of fraud or bilking to describe conduct.

Disease.

In the past allegations of venereal disease, typhoid, and leprosy were the stuff of which libel suits were made. Now of course, AIDS is the disease of the moment. Any allegation that someone has AIDS is defamatory. Therefore, the same rules apply.

Statements That Assert Inability to Conduct Lawful Occupation.

Examples: Lawyer is incompetent
Treasurer can't add.
Piano tuner is tone deaf.

Not defamatory: A carpenter is a hypocrite.

Sexual Conduct.

Reporting on sexual conduct is most dangerous. Even statements attributing sexual conduct that do not constitute crimes, but which violate local mores may subject you to liability. No one is prosecuted for cheating on a spouse or for being a homosexual. But to state that someone is cheating on a spouse, promiscuous, homosexual, perhaps even heterosexual if the person is homosexual could get you in trouble.

As the rules say, Sex is seldom safe!

Of and Concerning the Complainant.

One of the essential elements of a libelous statement is that it must be of and concerning the plaintiff. thus, one of the ways to avoid a sticky situation is to consider not naming or otherwise identifying a sticky subject.

However, identifying a subject can be done in more ways than by name. A rose by any other name would smell as sweet. Thus, you must consider the identifying information, not just the name when determining whether a defamatory statement could be attributed to the plaintiff.

Small towns have a more difficult time than metro areas. To say a high school senior in Detroit, does not identify anyone, but to say that a high school senior in Sanilac may in fact limit the pool of possibilities sufficiently to identify the subject.

Defamatory statements about small groups can be considered to refer to each member of the group. For example, the statement "a junior high school coach was charged with theft" could be a problem if there are only five coaches in the junior high. Identifying a group of at least 25 is safest. E.g. "An athletic coach in the tri-county area was charged with theft." Thus, a member of a small group can treat the defamatory statement about the small group as being a statement "of and concerning" that individual member.

Unprivileged Communication.

Certain communications are privileged provided they meet certain conditions. These include the absolute privilege to make a **fair and true** report of official proceedings and government actions, the so called official proceedings privilege. **(See Chapter Three, Reporters Privilege)**.

There is also the qualified privilege created by the case of **New York Times** v **Sullivan**, 376 US 254; 84 S Ct 710; 11 L Ed 2d 686 (1964), in which the U.S. Supreme Court held that public officials must prove that a statement was published with knowledge that it was false or with reckless disregard for the truth in order to recover in a libel action. This requirement of "actual malice" was based upon the recognition that even a false report about a public official has some value in a free society where public debate is to be encouraged. **(See Chapter Nine)** That qualified privilege extends to public **figures** as well.

If you determine that one of more of the figures in your story are public figures or public officials, which is often the case, you then must carefully examine your own state of mind with regard to the person. That is because the test becomes whether or not you had a subjective reason to believe that the report was false.

Obviously, a good journalist should never have to worry since suspicious facts should never make it into a story. But journalists are also human; sometimes a journalist loses perspective and fails to recognize facts which destroy the premise of the story that he or she has been working on for months.

Absolute and Qualified Privilege

Reporters rarely have absolute privilege as a protection from a libel action. However, it is accepted in our form of government that certain persons should be able to say whatever they feel or think, whether the statements are true or false in order to encourage open debate. The public is protected when talking to government. Congress members on the floor of Congress, state legislators in the state legislative chambers and persons appearing before a court of law, grand juries or administrative agencies are protected no matter what they say in disparaging remarks or maligning others. That is why Wisconsin Sen. Joseph McCarthy chose to make accusations about people being Communists on the floor of the U.S. Senate in the 1950's. City council members, mayors and high administrators also enjoy some protection. Lower level officials do not.[1] As discussed in another chapter, you are protected when you report the debate in the congress or testimony in court so long as your report is fair and accurate.

A False Statement of Fact.

Although many libel cases are decided on the basis of the public figure status of the plaintiff, truth is a complete defense to a libel action. Such a defense does much more for a newspaper's credibility than some of the defenses discussed above.

But what is truth? The lawyer in a courtroom quickly learns that "truth" is in large part perception, measured against probabilities as seen through a veil of persuasion.

Gerald Lindquist argued that he did not forge his daughter's signature because he had her permission to sign her name to the absentee vote application, a fact which she confirmed. But the state laws on voter qualifications do not allow the county clerk to accept such signatures and the statement "Lindquist forged Name" was held to be true.

Fortunately, the law of libel recognizes the nature of truth. Thus, a defendant in a libel case can defeat the libel claim if the offending statement is substantially true, or its corollary that the statement is not materially false. And often that escape can be made early in the case without expensive discovery.

To understand how truth can be used effectively to short circuit a libel lawsuit, it is important to revisit the basic elements of a libel/slander claim: 1) a false statement of fact which is 2) defamatory, 3) of and concerning the plaintiff, 4) unprivileged in its communication to a third party, and 5) negligently made.

Thus the first element of a libel claim is a false statement of fact. By allowing substantial truth to defeat a claim of libel the law allows the necessary breathing room to accommodate freedom of expression not to mention innocent error while offering protection to reputation in the extreme case. To put it another way the plaintiff must prove that the offending statement is substantially false, before the law will punish the speech of the defendant.

---

[1] ***Florida Media Law, 2nd edition, by Donna Lee Dickerson, University of South Florida Press, 1991.***

The Restatement of Torts puts it this way:

> Slight inaccuracies of expression are immaterial provided that the defamatory charge is true in substance.

Substantial Truth.

The Michigan Supreme Court recognized this principle as early as 1891 in the case of **McAllister v Detroit Free Press,** 85 Mich 453; 48 NW 612 (1891)**.** If the gist or the sting of the statement taken and considered in context is substantially true, there is no cause of action for libel. If the effect of the statements of which plaintiff complains on the reader is no different than the effect of the truth on the reader, there can be no action maintained for libel.

> It is sufficient for the defendant to justify so much of the defamatory matter as constitutes the sting of the charge, and it is unnecessary to repeat and justify every word of the alleged defamatory matter, so long as the substance of the libelous charge be justified...[A] slight inaccuracy in one of its details will not prevent the defendant's succeeding, providing the inaccuracy in no way alters the complexion of the affair, and would have no different effect on the reader than that which the literal truth would produce...**McAllister, at p. 460.**.

A recent case, **Koniak v Heritage Newspapers**, 198 Mich App 577; 499 NW2d 346 (1993) illustrates the application of this concept of substantial truth in two settings which are often the subject of libel suits: numbers and criminal charges. The plaintiff in **Koniak** sought damages for a report that his stepdaughter had complained to police that he had assaulted her 30 to 50 times. At the preliminary examination, the stepdaughter had testified that he had only assaulted her eight times.

The newspaper continued to report the earlier accusation of 30 to 50 incidents of abuse. When the criminal case against the plaintiff went to trial, it resulted in a verdict of not guilty.

The plaintiff sued claiming that the repetition of the allegations of 30 to 50 incidents of sexual abuse was false and defamatory, in light of the testimony at the preliminary exam that there were only eight incidents, and his acquittal.

But the Court of Appeals upheld the trial court's dismissal of the case because "the inaccurate statements reporting the criminal sexual conduct charges constituted minor differences that do not support a finding of material falsity." The court said that it agreed with the trial court that whether the plaintiff was alleged to have assaulted his step daughter once, eight times or thirty times "would have little effect on the reader." The Plaintiff's reputation was damaged regardless of the number of offenses claimed by his accuser. Since the report of the charge of abuse was not materially false, the report could not form the basis of a libel suit.

The plaintiff's second complaint revolved around the reporter's description of an assault and battery plea proceeding. The plaintiff pleaded nolo contendere to a charge of assault and battery against his wife. The newspaper reported his plea and followed it with the statement that the plaintiff was "willing to accept the consequences of the conviction." However, in fact, the plaintiff was not "convicted" because the judge in the criminal proceeding did not accept the plea but instead took the plea under advisement for six months.

Again the Court of Appeals affirmed the trial court's dismissal because it said "we cannot say that the article had a different effect upon the mind of the reader than would the literal truth...The article was substantially true, and would not tend to prejudice the plaintiff any more than a similar article using technically precise language describing the literal truth."

In other cases similar errors have been found insufficient to meet the mark of material falsity.

> **<u>Orr</u> v <u>Argus-Press Co.</u>, 586 F2d 1108 (6th Cir. 1978), certiorari denied 440 US 960, 99 S Ct 1502, 59 L Ed 2d 773.** Statements that plaintiffs actions were a "fraud" and a "swindle" and "a phony shopping mall investment" were substantially true reports of a 15 count indictment for violations of state securities laws.
>
> **<u>Fisher</u> v <u>Detroit Free Press, Inc.</u>,158 Mich App 409; 404 NW2d 765; 13 Med. L. Rptr. 2241 (1987).** Misstatement of amount of damages sought by plaintiff in original action had no different effect on the reader and thus could not be basis of libel action.
>
> **<u>Morganroth</u> v <u>Whitall</u>, 161 Mich App 785; 411 NW2d 859 (1987).** Newspaper's description of hairdresser as "blowtorch lady", "dressed for blow torching duty in a slashed-to-there white jumpsuit" was not actionable since statements were substantially true. The court said, `We have examined the photographic exhibits submitted by defendant at the motion hearing and we conclude that reasonable minds could not differ in reaching the conclusion that plaintiff did, in fact, wear a jumpsuit"slashed-to-there."'

In 1992 the Michigan Supreme Court decided the landmark case of **<u>Rouch</u> v <u>Enquirer & News of Battle Creek</u>, 440 Mich 238; 487 NW2d 205 (1992)**. In that opinion, known as <u>Rouch II</u> by reason of the prior appeal on different issues of libel law, the Supreme Court reversed a $1 million verdict because it found that the article was substantially true.

The Court concluded the <u>Rouch II</u> opinion as follows:

> We conclude that the evidence was not sufficient to establish **material falsity**. (emphasis supplied).

Reading the Statement in Context.

Statements must also be read in context. A libel plaintiff is not allowed to have the statement read in a void or out of context.. In 1886 the Michigan Supreme Court said:

> **The article, in order to try its libelous quality, must all be read together. Parts of it cannot be severed from the rest, so as to give them a meaning which the whole would not justify, and the spirit of the whole article must be determined largely from the occasion which led to it. Morganroth v Whitall, 161 Mich App 785; 411 NW2d 859 (1987).**

The Supreme Court affirmed this principle in the case of **Locricchio v Evening News Association, 438 Mich 84; 476 NW2d 112 (1991).** In the **Locricchio** case a jury found for the plaintiff not because of any misstatement of fact in a Detroit News series, but because the overall tone of the article might lead a reader to believe the plaintiff had connections with organized crime. The Michigan Supreme Court threw out the verdict and the U.S. Supreme Court refused to hear an appeal.

> Similarly, the headlines in the series, while arguably inflammatory do not convey false implications apart from the context of the reported facts...
>
> ...Again, however, the articles must be construed as a whole, and the article later pointed out that intensive investigations by law enforcement agencies failed to link the plaintiffs to the Leach (or Brush) murders. **Locricchio, supra, at 131**.

While the Detroit News eventually won the **Locricchio** case, legal observers say that was probably the most expensive libel case in Michigan legal history, costing millions of dollars to defend.

Good result; long time coming. But the Locricchio decision will make it easier for libel defendants to dismiss cases. The lesson of Locricchio is to be certain short, snappy headlines, picture captions and bullets are adequately explained in the body of the story.

Hyperbole.

A final wrinkle in the defense of truth is the defense of hyperbole or rhetoric. This defense is an extension of the argument that the plaintiff cannot prove that the statement is materially false.

Hyperbolic speech or rhetoric by definition is not capable of a materially false meaning. By hyperbolic speech we mean speech that is so outrageous, caustic, vituperative in the extreme, that is not provably false. Since the plaintiff cannot prove such speech to be probably false, the plaintiff's libel case must fail. Statements that cannot "reasonably be interpreted as stating actual facts" about an individual such as rhetorical hyperbole, are protected from libel actions.

In the premier case discussing hyperbole and rhetoric, (although not a libel case by the time it reached the U.S. Supreme Court) the plaintiff, the Rev. Jerry Falwell complained about a cartoon in Hustler magazine's parody issue that portrayed him as an incestuous drunk. **Hustler Magazine v Falwell, 485 US 46; 108 S Ct 876; 99 L Ed 2d 41; 56 U.S.L.W. 4180, (1988)**. The cartoon at issue was a parody of the Campari Liqueur ads. The ads had used the technique of double entendre, depicting famous persons talking about their "first time". Although the "first time" was ostensibly the first time that they had tried the liqueur, the double entendre was the implication that the description also applied to the first time they had a sexual experience.

The cartoon parody of Reverend Falwell suggested that his "first time" had been in an outhouse with his mother while he was drunk. Rev. Falwell did not laugh. But notwithstanding the distasteful nature of the Hustler cartoon, Justice Rehnquist writing for the Supreme Court declined to uphold liability. He described the need to protect such speech as follows.

> **The sort of robust political debate encouraged by the First Amendment is bound to produce speech that is critical of those who hold public office or those public figures who are "intimately involved in the resolution of important public questions or, by reason of their fame, shape events in areas of concern to society at large. "Justice Frankfurter put it succinctly ... when he said that "one of the prerogatives of American citizenship is the right to criticize public men and measures." Such criticism, inevitably will not always be reasoned or moderate; public figures as well as public officials will be subject to "vehement, caustic, and sometimes unpleasantly sharp attacks."** Hustler Magazine, at p.50.

As a result of this analysis, Falwell was denied recovery because he had been unable to demonstrate that Hustler had made a false statement of fact about him and the Court would not punish even outrageous speech without a showing of a false statement of fact. The ad after all had been clearly identified as parody.

Even if the individual is not a public figure, courts have generally held that epithets and insults are not defamatory. This is because such expressions are not capable of conveying false facts. An allegation that some one is a "turkey" for example, really expresses no fact. It only indicates that the speaker does not hold them in high regard.

Other examples of hyperbole and rhetoric which have been successfully defended include the following name calling: "horse's ass" or that an idea was "cockamamie" or that someone was a "bastard" or a "scab" or like Hitler, a sleezebag, Mexican mafia. Statements found not to be protected as hyperbole include descriptions of actions as "scamming" or "bilking".

Hyperbole and rhetorical speech are historically part of First Amendment protections. Whenever especially critical speech is attacked as being libelous, one should consider whether the speech is sufficiently caustic to fall within this category of speech which cannot be proven false.

Opinion.

There is more protection for speech which is seen as opinion than for speech which is seen as a statement of fact. The problem is that legal distinctions between the two occupy volumes of case law. For the reporter, it is best to leave the protection of the opinion privilege to the editorial page. Although a lawyer may assert opinion as a defense to a libel claim, it is not a privilege that will generally be useful to a reporter in writing a story.

However, there are times when the opinion privilege will be useful. Another incarnation of the opinion privilege is the concept of fair comment. Thus, if you are reporting both sides of a controversy and each side contains some defamatory statements about the other, you may safely report on these defamatory matters provided that the reporting is clear to indicate there is no endorsement of the truth of the defamatory positions - of either side.

The opinion privilege has not been considered by a Michigan appellate court since the U.S. Supreme Court decision rejecting a formal opinion privilege as a matter of constitutional law. **Milkovich v Lorain Journal Co., 497 US 1; 110 S Ct 2695; 111 L Ed 2d 1, (1990)**. However, Justice Boyle has recognized the importance of Fair Comment which is really another formulation of the opinion privilege.

Certainly opinions expressed on the Opinion Page enjoy a large measure of protection from the Courts, especially if there is a political opinion involved. However, reporters should be careful about opinions in a news story, unless all sides of the controversy are given room to speak. And even then, defamatory statements of fact should not be included. These are often situations in which hyperbole can be useful.

Chapter 2

Check List for Invasion of Privacy

1. **The classic complaint consists of publication of private facts, concerning the plaintiff, which are highly offensive to a reasonable person and of no legitimate concern to the public.**

2. **Medical facts are usually considered to be private facts.**

3. **News articles, advertisements, photos and letters to the editor all should be examined for possible invasion of privacy.**

4. **If you got the private information from public documents they should not be able to successfully sue you. Your defense is the fair and true report of a government document.**

5. **The best defense is to get a waiver from individuals. This is particularly true of photographs.**

6. **You should obtain permission from the resident before you go on private property in pursuit of photos or a story. It is not sufficient to get the permission of a governmental agency like the police or of a non-resident owner of the property.**

7. **Don't run embarrassing information or pictures of private individuals unless there is a compelling news purpose. And then do it with great care.**

8. **Interviewing or taking pictures of children is particularly risky. Try to always clear these with a responsible parent.**

9. **Make sure you believe there is a public interest in knowing the name of an individual involved in an incident as well as the facts of the incident.**

Chapter 2

Invasion of Privacy

It is possible to get it right and still be in trouble. The privacy rights of individuals about whom you write can trump the journalist's best story. And if as a reporter you lie, cheat, steal, secretly record or pose as someone you are not you are at risk of winding up in court on some sort of invasion of privacy claim. We're not saying you should never do it, but never do it without express permission of the top supervising editor in your newsroom.

An individual citizen's right to privacy is basically a 20th century concept that is growing more important year by year as news media outlets deliberately censor themselves on running some information and the citizenry gets more aggressive about protecting what they perceive to be their rights. In the past two decade in Michigan editors and reporters have deliberately begun leaving some information out of news reports thus expanding the public concept of what is private and should be left out of the media.

"The Right of Privacy" was first proposed by Louis Brandeis, later to be a U.S. Supreme Court justice and Samuel Warren in a Harvard Law Review article in 1890. Four types of invasion of privacy: appropriation, intrusion, false light and publication of private information were identified by William Prosser in 1965 as part of his book, Restatement of Torts.

The most important defense to a claim of privacy rights is that the identity of the individual as well as the facts are newsworthy. When in doubt, get permission from the person to use her name or don't identify the person.

When reporting crimes, the alleged perpetrator's identity is always newsworthy. The identity of the victim probably is if the police will give it to you. But witnesses' identities may be more touchy assuming you can get access to their names.

Ask yourself the question: "Is the identity of this person important to my readers for a fair understanding of this story?"

Reporters and editors need to know what information they can legally print under Michigan and U.S. law and publishers need to decide what legal information they are willing to print and ask themselves why or why not print it. For example: most newspapers no longer print the addresses of crime victims, witnesses, or those attending a wedding or funeral ceremony. The perception--real or unreal--is that criminals might take advantage of that information to inflict further harm on individuals or rob those folks they know are not at home. That doesn't take into account that any truly bad person can look up the addresses of most people in the telephone book or in a cross reference directory at a local library.

At one time newspapers ran lists of divorces, the police blotter items with details on the victim and the culprit or suspect, who was buying and selling real estate, and in some instances even a "johns" list, so-called because it gave name and addresses of men arrested for soliciting prostitutes in a public service attempt to drive such transactions off the streets of certain communities.

Not much of that information survives in most newspapers except the price of real estate is listed in some. Some Michigan newspapers have extended their self-censoring to eliminating the exact location where a crime occurred. Others identify the location only by block number.

If as a reporter you feel compelled to go anywhere and do anything to get a story sooner or later you will run the risk of being charged with criminal trespass. There is no First Amendment or Michigan legal protection from trespass laws. Various courts have held secret tape recording, breaking and entering or using trickery to gain admission to a private area are impermissible, intrusive methods of news gathering. If you are a photographer for the Cement City Chronicle and you ride with the engines to the scene of a fire at the Scrooge estate and Mr. Scrooge or a fire or police official tells you to get off the property you had better go.

While privately owned stores, shopping malls and parking lots are open to the public, if an owner can ask a member of the public to leave, he can ask a journalist to leave. This holds true also for private areas within public facilities such as jails, hospitals and schools.

Journalists posing as someone they are not is legal as long as it is not a ruse for trespass. For example if you pose as a hospital orderly so you can get in to interview a bedridden serial murder suspect you could be charged with criminal trespass. Posing as someone you are not may violate the ethics policy of the station or publication you work for, but it is not necessarily illegal. That is a decision for your editors to make. When two reporters for The Detroit News posed as executive secretaries for Burroughs, a prominent Detroit company, without permission while checking for racial discrimination by landlords renting apartments their editors made them go out and do fresh reporting before running the piece because of their false claims that they were working for a company other than the News . And two ABC television news producers found that lying on job applications at a Food Lion store in the south caused jurors to agree on a multi-million dollar verdict against the network.

Most news agencies today would err on the side of being up front with sources rather than gain information by trickery or subterfuge and damage the credibility of the publication or station. But there are times when such techniques are useful. However, there can be liability.

Photographers pose particular questions. In general, the right to photograph depends on whether public or private property is involved and, more specifically, whether the people inside are entitled to privacy. A photographer needs permission to enter a home and also to take pictures there, but they may photograph anyone in public areas, such as parks, streets, or a sporting stadium. Taking pictures from a public place is not illegal, even if it is picture of a home owner at his front door or in the window, if the photographer is curbside, but telephoto lenses or night lenses often strike juries as unfair and an invasion of privacy.

The death of Princess Diana has raised questions of the role of the press in obtaining facts about public figures, facts which the public figures wish to keep private. Of course, leaving a well known restaurant does not qualify as a private fact. Therefore there is no rightful legal claim for invasion of privacy. Nor is it an embarrassing fact. However, even if there were an embarrassing fact such as drunkenness or nudity or something of the like, in leaving the restaurant, if the conduct occurred in a public place, it does not qualify for a privacy claim because it is not a private fact. Public drunkenness is embarrassing but is not a private fact; leaving a secluded restaurant may be a private fact but is not usually embarrassing. So again it will not fulfill the elements of a claim for invasion of privacy.

There is no invasion of privacy without both elements: private fact and embarrassing or highly offensive fact.

Even if both of these elements is met, there is the last element: newsworthiness. In the case of Gary Hart, his activities on board a boat with a model were private facts and embarrassing, but they were newsworthy. Therefore, Gary Hart had no cause of action for invasion of privacy.

But even though there maybe no claim for invasion of privacy, that does not bar a claim of trespass or assault.

In the case of Princess Diana and other popular celebrities the public desire for photographs of them has led to extraordinary means to obtain photographs often without regard for privacy interests of the objects of the quest. But if those extraordinary means violate the law, for example speeding, dangerous driving, and in the most tragic of cases death, the inquiry has nothing to do with the press and everything to do with the laws of the land with regard to such conduct

Do not expect to wrap yourself in the First Amendment if you have flat out violated the law - left the scene of an accident, speeding, refused to obey an officer's legitimate request for you to move, parked in a no parking zone or trespassed. There are no special privileges for news gathering. The right of access is the same for the press as it is for the public. What is given to the press is the privilege of using the rights granted to all citizens in this country to have access to government so that they may be an informed electorate.

Therefore, criminal conduct - causing an accident, trespassing, posing as a police officer and misrepresentations - lying on an application to Food Lion, are not going to be protected by the First Amendment. There is a difference between what is inappropriate or distasteful conduct or the ends justifies the means and illegal conduct. It may have been tacky to take a picture of

Diana in a see-through skirt with the light behind her; it is quite another to force her car into a bridge abutment to get a photograph. Forcing a car off the road is illegal regardless of the motive.

The Food Lion case offers many important lessons for the press. If you lie to get into areas that are private and obtain embarrassing or offensive facts, there are legal consequences. After all the ABC crew could have taken their concerns to government agencies and then made FOIA requests for the results of those investigations. They could have published interviews with workers about the conditions. If Food Lion sued them for libel, ABC would have had the power of court subpoenas and the right of access under the legal system to the very areas they obtained access to surreptitiously. Utilizing lies and deceit were not the only avenue open to the reporters and editors in this case to get this story.

If there was concern that state investigators were corrupt or incompetent, there are federal investigators and others who are trained to undertake these kinds of investigations. Undercover work has its pitfalls. Of course, Food Lion in a very clever move did not sue for libel or invasion of privacy. It sued for fraud, pure and simple. Although this case is playing itself through the court, the press must remember that as the eyes and ears of the public, it has no more rights than the public of which those eye and ears are a part. The press is subject to the same limitations on its conduct as the average citizen. What the First Amendment recognizes is the importance of the existence of the press to exercise the rights of citizens to have access to information so that they can speak knowledgeably about the world around them.

Areas open to the public for a specific purpose such as a restaurant can pose problems. One court held that diners have a reasonable expectation of peace in a restaurant and thus a photographer must ask permission to photograph them.

Accompanying the police to a suspect's home does not give a photographer the right to take pictures inside the home. When filming police activities photographers would be wise to remain on the street and film the suspects from there rather than following the police into the suspect's home. The film should be carefully edited to exclude photos of innocent people and to specifically identify the suspect. Courts have rejected the theory that reporters and photographers gain authority to enter private property by being in the company of police. The right of police to enter a dwelling does not extend to inviting the press to come with them.

It should be kept in mind that the privilege to publish information gained by means of trespass is an independent question. Even though the journalist's conduct might be punishable as trespass, the publication of the information is measured by a different standard. In the Food Lion case the producers were found guilty of trespass and fraud for lying on job applications rather than for airing anything libelous. In any event, a journalist must balance the right and need to get the information against the right of privacy and other public interests.[1]

---

[1] "Legally Speaking" Michigan Press Association Bulletin No. 19. Dawn Phillips, 1991.

The Detroit News was sued by an agency executive who allowed a photographer to take pictures of her in front of battered mothers and their children playing in the background. The photographer assured the official the children and their moms would not be identifiable when the picture appeared. His editor confirmed that view when the agency exec telephoned her concerns before publication. However, when the picture appeared it was one of the best cases of color reproduction to that point that had appeared in The News and the Board of Directors of the shelter for abused families fired the official. She collected a settlement from The News. The moral: don't make promises you can't keep. If innocent children or bystanders are involved in a sensitive story make sure their rights of privacy are protected.

Nor is the advertising department safe from claims of invasion of privacy. Just as advertising departments must watch for libel they must also look for ads which may invade privacy, either because they contain private facts or because they misappropriate someone's likeness to sell a product. The tort of invasion of privacy also includes the tort of misappropriation of one's likeness for a commercial purpose without permission. Here the key is permission, not newsworthiness. If MacDonald's tried to capitalize on a picture of Michael Jackson eating MacDonald's fries by placing his picture in their advertisements without his permission, they could be sued for misappropriation.

You may have noticed that in this general introduction to privacy we have talked about trespass, private facts and misappropriation. We have not mixed apples and oranges.

Privacy rights come in several forms: publication of embarrassing, private facts; Intrusion; misappropriation; false light; Constitutional right of privacy. Let's look at each of these interests.

Publication of embarrassing, private facts

The classic invasion of privacy tort consists of publication of private, albeit true, facts; of and concerning the plaintiff; which are highly offensive to a reasonable person; and which are of no legitimate concern to the public, i.e. not "newsworthy".

There is the common law concept of privacy which means that damages can be awarded for the publication of truly private facts, the disclosure of which would be offensive to a reasonable person. This is the classic invasion of privacy tort.

Types of facts considered to be private include some of the same categories haunted by libel plaintiffs such as professional misconduct, disease, criminal conduct and sexual conduct, but also include other less suspecting categories as relatives, job performance, and compromising situations.

Thus, if you discover the mayor has a retarded son in a state institution for retarded children, a fact that is known only to members of the immediate family, you may be found liable for damages for printing the true fact as an invasion of privacy.

In one case a woman claimed invasion of privacy for a photograph of her exiting a carnival fun house showing her with her skirt blown up over her head. Although the plaintiff's face was obscured the picture clearly showed her underwear and the faces of the rest of her family. Plaintiff's attendance at the carnival was not a private fact, but her undergarments were. This points out again that a newspaper is responsible for everything which appears in its pages from photos and editorials to letters to the editor and news articles.

As the Court in that case said, a person who's part of a public scene like a carnival or a baseball game may be photographed lawfully and the picture published as an incidental part of the scene. But if the individual suddenly finds himself in an unexpected, embarrassing situation he may have a right of privacy. Or put another way, if misfortune overtakes an individual in a public place, they are not necessarily fare game for your camera.

So watch out for the picture of the unsuspecting baseball fan picking his nose or kissing his girlfriend. Her mother may be watching!

In a case a few years ago, an advertisement was placed in a newspaper:

> **Don't bear the heartbreak of chlamydia alone. Chlamydia can cause sterility. Call 123-4567, 24 hours a day for more information.**

123-4567 was the telephone number of the plaintiff. She had chlamydia and sued the newspaper and her old boyfriend for placing the ad. This was a private fact, a medical condition presumably known to her, her doctor and apparently the boy friend. The newspaper escaped liability because on its face the ad did not alert the newspaper of plaintiff's identity. But such an ad raises concern. Classified ads must be watched closely. Newspapers have been sued over similar ads placed as practical jokes.

Sexual conduct is an area which requires <u>extreme caution</u>. The Michigan Court of Appeals has held that sexual conduct is private conduct, the disclosure of which can constitute invasion of privacy.

The trump card for invasion of privacy claims even of private embarrassing facts is newsworthiness. Thus the reports of Gary Hart's frolic on the waves with Donna Rice were protected speech because, although the activities were private and embarrassing, they were newsworthy by reason of Candidate Hart's protestations of fidelity in his marriage, not to mention his invitation for scrutiny.

The Michigan Court has also indicated what it thinks constitutes newsworthy material, notwithstanding potentially embarrassing facts. In **<u>Porter</u>** v **<u>City of Royal Oak</u>, 214 Mich App 478; 542 NW2d 905 (1995),** the Court of Appeals rejected the claims of a police officer that his privacy had been invaded when the City released the charges against him. The charges had been sustained through all appeals and through a lawsuit. Yet when Royal Oak released the charges to the media, the police officer claimed his right of privacy had been invaded. The Court in rejecting his claim set forth this description of what is newsworthy:

> **Included within the scope of legitimate public concerns are matters of the kind customarily regarded as "news." To a considerable extent, in accordance with the mores of the community, the publishers and broadcasters have themselves defined the term, as a glance at any morning newspaper will confirm. Authorized publicity includes publications concerning homicide and other crimes, arrests, police raids, suicides, marriages and divorces accidents, fires, catastrophes of nature, a death from the use of narcotics, a rare disease, the birth of a child to a 12-year-old girl, the reappearance of one supposed to have been murdered years ago, a report to the police concerning the escape of a wild animal and many other similar matters of genuine, even if more or less deplorable, popular appeal. (Winstead v Sweeney, 205 Mich App 664, 669; 517 NW2d 874 (1994) quoting 3 Restatement, Torts, 2d § 652D, comment g, pp. 390-391).**

Good journalism is the rule. Ask the question: How will this person's identity or picture assist the reader in understanding the story?

Intrusion

Another aspect of privacy is the publication of private facts not even necessarily embarrassing but which are obtained by intrusion. This cause of action is akin to trespass. It often arises when a reporter finds herself some place where she has no legal right to be: a hospital room, a private home albeit in the company of the police, a doctor's office, a psychiatrist's file room.

It is the procuring of information by intruding into someone's private space. The information may be true, may be newsworthy and yet the tort of intrusion will still prevail. Newsworthiness is not a defense. Nor is publication of the facts gathered necessary to support a claim for intrusion

.

> **One who intentionally intrudes, physically, or otherwise, upon the solitude or seclusion of another or his private affairs or concerns, is subject to liability to the other for invasion of his privacy, if the intrusion would be highly offensive to a reasonable person.**[2]

Claims of intrusion have become more common with more aggressive reporting. Hidden cameras, posing as a doctor to gain access to a hospital, and similar activities have lead to these kinds of claims.

---

[2] Restatement (Second) of Torts § 652B (1977).

Photographs can intrude as well. So long as the photograph was taken or could have been taken by standing in an area open to the public, there is no problem. But beware of the invitation by someone other than the occupant of the premises.

The most important aspect to understand about intrusion is that consent is the only defense. And the police or other authorities cannot supply you with that consent. Only the owner of the premises can give you consent to be on private property. If you go on private property at the invitation of the police or the fire department and the owner asks you to leave, leave if you want to avoid any possible conflict.

There are several circumstances which may give rise to an intrusion claim including: Gaining information through false pretenses, exceeding the consent given for entry, theft or trespass.

One of the more famous intrusion cases is that of Jackie Onassis. A photographer, Mr. Galella made a career out of following her and photographing her. When she sued, he argued that she had created a cult following out of herself and shouldn't complain. But the Court ordered him to stay at least 90 feet away and several years later found him in contempt for violating that order.

Reporters and photographers must also beware and be mindful of the orders of police and firemen to move back. Failure to obey these orders of police authorities can lead to arrest and prosecution and the First Amendment offers no protection.

Reporters for Reuters and the Michigan Daily were arrested for failure to obey directions from authorities and resisting arrest. The First Amendment was no defense. The reporters had to rely upon proving that in fact they had obeyed the orders. Fortunately there was video footage showing both reporters well within the designated area. The police had overstepped their bounds. But that ability of the reporters to avoid criminal sanctions rested upon the reporters' ability to prove that their conduct was lawful and that they followed directions, not because they were protected by the First Amendment.

False Light

False light means to characterize someone in a demeaning, embarrassing or otherwise inappropriate manner. The distinguishing feature of this claim is that it hurts feelings not necessarily reputations.

In our litigious society false light claims can range from a hair stylist, who used a blowtorch for her creative tool to an attorney who felt a newspaper suggested he was keeping company with a tree.

In her .article “Legal Developments” Alice Neff Lucan, formerly a Gannett attorney, and Sheila R. Caudle wrote about a case that took years to work through the Michigan legal system.

`One day a Chevy smashed into the oak tree that stood on the land of Troy, Michigan attorney William Fisher. Seeking "whatever legal damages in excess of $10,000 the court deems just," he filed suit against the driver, the car's owner and the car's insurer, claiming that the car damaged his "beautiful oak tree".' [3]

While a court dismissed the action under Michigan's no fault insurance law, Fisher appealed and in 1983 the Michigan Court of Appeals in a decision by Judge John H. Gillis opined:

> **We thought that we would never see**
> **A suit to compensate a tree.**
> **A suit whose claim in tort is prest**
> **Upon a mangled tree's behest;**
> **A tree whose battered trunk was prest**
> **Against a Chevy's crumpled crest;**
> **A tree that faces each new day**
> **With bark and limb in disarray;**
> **A tree that may forever bear**
> **A lasting need for tender care.**
> **Flora lovers though we three,**
> **We must uphold the court's decree.**
> **Affirmed.**

Fisher v Detroit Free Press, 158 Mich App 409; 404 NW2d 765; 13 Med. L. Rpt. 2241 (1987).

This bit of lyrical doggerel came to the attention of the Free Press and a reporter interviewed Gillis, quoted the poem and then added: 'The car's insurer offered to pay the tree surgeon's bill--$550--but Fisher sought $15,000 for the equivalent of "loss of companionship of the sick tree," Gillis said.'

Fisher then filed suit against the Free Press alleging defamation, invasion of privacy, unwarranted intrusion, false light publicity, public disclosure of private facts and wrongful appropriation of Fisher's name.

He contended the report falsely made it appear that he keeps a tree for a companion. He sought damages for his insulted honor and wounds to his pride and manly feelings.

A mediation panel recommended a zero award for Fisher, but Fisher pursued his case in court and when a judge granted summary judgment for the Free Press he appealed again. This time the Free Press filed a counter suit for actual and punitive damages against Fisher on ground

---

[3] "LEGAL Developments" Alice Neff Lucan and Sheila R. Caudle, "Decision in Detroit is Poetry to Libel Defendants" (Fisher v. Detroit Free Press, 158 Mich App 409; 404 NW2d 765; 13 Med. L. Rptr. 2241(1987).

that his appeal was meritless and vexatious. The Court of Appeals agreed and ordered Fisher to pay $6,262.55 in attorneys' fees.[4]

The moral of all that is that you can safely quote a judge's opinion, but that doesn't prevent someone from filing suit because of it.

Gillis was also involved in another bizarre case before a three judge panel in the Court of Appeals. That one also decided in 1987 pitted a suburban Detroit hairdresser, who used a blow torch to style hair while wearing a "jumpsuit slashed to there."

The story which treated the subject humorously under the headline "Hot Locks: Let Shila burn you a new "do" in the Detroit News Sunday magazine supplement also suggested the woman styled the hair of canines including her own dog.

Shila Morganroth sued for libel and invasion of privacy by false light. The trial court granted summary disposition and Ms. Morganroth subjected herself to Gillis' wit by appealing. Gillis concluded:

> ". . .Although the manner in which the present article was written may have singed plaintiff's desire for obtaining favorable coverage of her unique hairdressing methods, we cannot subscribe to the view that it was libelous. We believe that the trial court aptly summarized this case when it stated that "this Court is of the Opinion that the Plaintiff sought publicity and got it." Indeed, it would appear that the root of plaintiff's dissatisfaction with defendant's article is that the publicity plaintiff received was not exactly the publicity she had in mind. While the publicity may have been inflammatory from plaintiff's vantage point, we do not believe it was libelous. At most, defendants treated the article more lightheartedly than plaintiff either anticipated or hoped. While this may give plaintiff cause to cancel her subscription to the Detroit News, it does not give her cause to complain in court. Affirmed. Costs to defendants" **Morganroth v Whitall, 161 Mich App 785, 794; 411 NW2d 859 (1987).**

Another example of a potential false light claim that probably will not succeed, is a claim of false light because someone has been identified with the wrong political party. During election years it is common to receive political ads with a list of persons identified as supporters of the candidate. No signatures are offered and even if they were how is a newspaper to know they are genuine. In a recent case alleging false light claims the Michigan courts have described the claim as follows:

> **In order to maintain an action for false light invasion of privacy, a plaintiff must show that the defendant broadcast to the public in general, or to a large number of people, information that was unreasonable and highly**

4 Ibid.

objectionable by attributing the plaintiff characteristics, conduct, or beliefs that were false and place the plaintiff in a false position. <u>Duran</u> v <u>Detroit News</u>, 200 Mich App 622, 631-632; 504 NW2d 715 (1993).

However, common sense suggests that you review a list of supporters for persons unlikely to support a candidate just as you should review letter writer signers to make sure no one is playing a practical joke on someone with public and controversial views on subjects such as abortion, animal rights or the environment.

Misappropriation

This usually deals with advertising when an advertiser or advertising sales person decides to run a picture of a famous person or even a private citizen in an advertisement without that person's consent. However, it can impinge on the editorial department, for example, when a photographer shoots a great picture at a public event and the newspaper decides to turn it into a poster. That is what happened in the case of the 1984 Word Series when Tigers hero Kirk Gibson won a game with a decisive homer and rounded the bases in an emotional charge. Photographer Mary Schroeder's classic picture dominated the front page of the Free Press the next day and captured the attention of Tigers fans everywhere. So some promotion genius had the idea to turn it into a poster. A great idea, but not without Gibson's consent. He sued.

Constitutional Right of Privacy

The Courts have recognized that there are certain zones of privacy for the individual. It is often referred to as the right to be left alone. This concept is important to understand because it sometimes is used to measure whether or not something is private.

The constitutional right of privacy is limited in scope and applicability. First, it is limited to restricting government activity, not the activity of private citizens or reporters. Moreover, constitutional privacy is limited to narrow zones of privacy consisting of procreation and abortion.

In **<u>Doe</u> v <u>Mills</u>, 212 Mich App 73; 536 NW2d 824 (1995),** the Michigan Court of Appeals considered the liability of the defendants who had gone through the garbage of an abortion clinic, learned the names of Jane Doe and other plaintiffs who planned to have abortions and placed their names on posters which were displayed as part of a demonstration against the clinic. In rejecting the Plaintiffs' constitutional claims of invasion of privacy the court comprehensively reviewed so-called "Constitutional privacy." At the outset, the Court noted that "(t)he constitutional right of privacy is not to be equated with the common law right (to privacy) recognized by state tort law.", <u>Id</u>. citing **<u>McNally</u> v <u>Pulitzer Publishing Co</u>, 532 F2d 69, 76 (CA 8, 1976)**. As opposed to creating expansive new rights the **<u>Doe</u>** ruling noted that the Fourth Amendment has been explicitly interpreted by the U.S. Supreme Court as providing a different sort of privacy protection than that afforded by individual states" law:

(T)he Fourth Amendment cannot be translated into a general constitutional "right of privacy." That Amendment protects individual privacy against certain kinds of governmental intrusion, but its protections go further, ***and often have nothing to do with privacy at all.*** **Other provisions of the Constitution protect personal privacy from other forms of governmental invasion. But the protection of a person's general right to privacy--his right to be let alone by other people--is, like the protection of his property and of his very life, left largely to the law of the individual States. Doe, 212 Mich App at 86; 536 NW2d, at 831; citing Katz v United States, 389 US 347, 350-351; 88 S Ct 507, 510-511; 19 L Ed 2d 576 (1967) (emphasis added).**

Constitutional privacy will affect news gathering in situations where you are seeking information in the possession of the government that is about individuals. The government will be loathe to give out information about individuals which the individuals may deem to be protected by notions of privacy. However, even then there is a distinction between common law invasion of privacy concerning private embarrassing facts and constitutional privacy which limits government action in regulating the conduct or even collecting the information.

Waiver

Your best defense is to get a waiver or permission to use facts which are potentially embarrassing that you obtain from an individual or get the subjects to sign releases for photographs.

Children

Reporting on children is always a bit risky. There is little law in the area of invasion of privacy for children. The problem comes in because they are minors and are therefore not capable of giving permission, for example, to have their picture taken or to be quoted.

On the other hand, the statute of limitations on other torts does not begin to run until the child turns eighteen. Thus, can a parent give permission for photographing a child? What if the child feels the parent acted too hastily? Does the child have a right to sue once the child turns eighteen for the publication of an embarrassing private fact years before. There are no answers, but permission of the parent is essential to your legal safety.

In short, be careful about publishing facts about children that could prove to be embarrassing or private. Of course, for the most part reporters are only writing about matters that are of legitimate public concern. Therefore any claim of privacy would be easily defeated, in theory at least.

Government Documents

Another defense is that the information is contained in legally obtained government documents. B.J.F., whose identity was protected throughout her case, was denied relief for the publication of her full name by a newspaper that she was the victim of a rape. The court declined to hold the newspaper liable even though the police had a policy of not releasing the names of rape victims. The police accidentally released the name. And the paper had a policy of not publishing such names, but a summer intern wrote the story and no one caught it.

The Florida statute which made it illegal to print the name of a rape victim was held unconstitutional because it punished the publication of information gotten legally from the government. **Florida Star v BJF, 491 US 524; 109 S Ct 2603; 16 Med. L. Rptr. 1801 (1989).**

Newsworthiness

In the recent Michigan case above which did not involve a newspaper the scope of the newsworthiness defense became critical. In **Doe, supra.**, the two anti-abortion protesters were not permitted to obtain dismissal of a privacy claim on the basis of newsworthiness for the publication of the real names of Jane Doe and Sally Roe on signs outside the Woman's Advisory Center in Livonia. The signs indicated that Doe and Roe were about to undergo abortions and implored them, inter alia, not to "kill their babies"

Plaintiffs made the necessary allegations that they did not give defendants permission to publicize the fact of their abortions. And that it was their intent to "keep the fact of their abortions private, confidential and free from any publicity." Plaintiff therefore sued the protesters for public disclosure of private facts. There was no allegation of falsity, just publication of private facts.

The Court noted an important distinction which must be kept in mind. Although the subject matter may be of legitimate public interest, an individual's involvement may not be of legitimate public concern. Thus although the public may be interested in the topic of abortion and abortion clinics and the protests related thereto, the public does not necessarily have a legitimate interest in the fact that these two specific individuals were consulting with an abortion clinic. If the fact is private, great care must be taken.

This is what makes the law of privacy so dangerous for a reporter. You may get the facts right and yet because they are accurate and private, there may be liability for an invasion of privacy. The **Doe** case is troublesome, but not unexpected.

So in evaluating a privacy concern consider the newsworthy nature of the facts separately from the newsworthy nature of the participant's name.

Whose Privacy Is it Anyway?

Only the living may sue for the protection of their right of privacy. There is no right of the estate or the family to sue for someone who is deceased. Death of a plaintiff requires dismissal of the case. However, care must be taken not to invade the privacy rights of the family and friends around the decedent.

In a case involving the suicide of a judge in Detroit, the family sued for invasion of privacy for the release of the autopsy which revealed that the judge had drugs in his blood at the time of his death. The Court of Appeals affirmed the dismissal of the case noting that the family had no right of privacy for the information about the deceased. However, the Court did caution that the family had the right to protect their own privacy. But nothing in the report on the judge's death or the autopsy infringed on the rights of any member of the family and none would be inferred.

Care should be taken even when the subject is deceased. Again recent events have heightened public concern over rights of privacy. In Michigan the legislature recently passed a statute forbidding the photographing of a dead body or body part in a grave or under water where recovery of the remains is not feasible. Although it is not clear who has the right to enforce a violation of the rights, it would appear that the estate of a deceased individual and thus his heirs would have a cause of action against the photograph of a dead body or parts of a dead body. Of course, body would have to be identifiable in order for a particular family to sue. However, there are also criminal penalties for photographing dead bodies or grave sites that show a dead body or a portion thereof. The statute was introduced after a Canadian Film crew took a submarine down to the site of the wreck of the Edmund Fitzgerald, a freighter of some fame and notoriety, which sank during a storm in the Great Lakes with the loss of the crew. Songs have been written and many documentaries done. However, in the recent filming there was what appeared to be a picture of an arm. Outraged family members of the crew took their concerns to the legislature. When Michigan Press Association suggested that this legislation was unnecessary, it met vehement opposition.

This statute undoubtedly will have little impact on every day journalism. But it sends a message of the attitude toward privacy these days. The folks who sought the legislation and who passed the legislation are the same folks who populate a jury in a case charging an invasion of privacy. This statute is a reminder of public sentiment.

In conclusion, even if a fact is true, you must also determine whether or not it is a private - 0POfact, an embarrassing fact and whether or not it is newsworthy.

Chapter 3

Reporter's Privilege Check List

1. Michigan's shield law protects a reporter from disclosing information to a grand jury that has been obtained confidentially from a source unless a defendant faces life imprisonment if convicted or the information can't be obtained by any other means and the judge deems it essential.

2. The courts have also recognized a newsman's privilege not to disclose confidential information to a third party litigant without a showing the information is essential and can be obtained by no other means.

3. Generally judges will quash subpoenas when a newspaper's attorney can show that the information can be obtained elsewhere.

4. A broadcaster is immune from prosecution on libel charges when he or she has given a political candidate use of the station to exercise rights under the Federal Communications Commission's Equal Time rules.

5. Federal law protects news rooms from searches and reporter's notes from seizure except under unusual circumstances. The exceptions are if the prosecutor believes the material will be destroyed if a subpoena is issued or if the seizure is necessary to prevent bodily injury to a citizen.

6. Your newspaper should have a consistent policy on destroying reporter notes. Various media outlets save them for set periods of time ranging from a week to a year. But whatever the policy all staffers should follow it. Having no policy or not consistently acting on one is legally dangerous.

7. If someone wants to serve you with a subpoena, accept it. Don't try to hide unless a supervisor tells you to do it.

8. Most subpoenas simply want you to verify the details in your story. Your editors will decide whether the news organization will cooperate or attempt to convince the court that you can simply sign an affidavit as to what appeared in print.

9. In case of a subpoena or search contact your supervisors and let them decide on a course of action.

10. Confidential sources present special problems and obligations; promise confidentiality only after very careful consideration.

Chapter 3

Privilege, Subpoenas and Searches

Reporters do not have a special privilege to access information not available to the public generally. Nor do they have the right to obtain information illegally by trespass or theft or disobeying police officers without the prospect of facing criminal prosecution. [1]

Reporters do have some protection however when it comes to being compelled to testify or produce documents. For example, Michigan's shield law (**MCL 767.5a; MSA 28.945 (1)**) protects both broadcast and print reporters from disclosing information to a grand jury that has been obtained confidentially from a source. However, this privilege does not apply to cases in which a defendant faces life imprisonment if convicted of the charges and other sources for the information have been exhausted and the information is deemed essential. Grand juries are groups of citizens brought together by a prosecutor to determine whether there is sufficient evidence to indict someone for a crime. If they believe there is enough evidence for a conviction they will authorize the prosecutor to issue an indictment. Their records are confidential so no stigma will attach to a citizen simply because he or she was investigated by a grand jury. [2]

Likewise, the courts have also recognized a "news writers privilege" not to disclose confidential information to a third party litigant without a showing that the requested information goes to the heart of the case and the litigant has exhausted all other means of obtaining the information. [3] Even if a confidential source is not at issue, some courts will quash (the legal term for revoke) subpoenas if the testimony is not necessary or will at least limit the questions that be asked. The reason for resisting all but the most compelling subpoenas, is that testifying either by deposition or at trial is a time consuming process. Attorneys and courts march to the beat a different drummer. Spending time testifying takes away from time needed to research and write new stories. Although some argue that reporters should have a sense of civic duty and testify, the nature of a reporter's work makes her more likely than the average civic minded citizen to subpoena. Too many subpoenas can seriously compromise a reporter's time and efforts.

Moreover, Michigan Rules of Evidence allow the introduction of newspaper articles without someone to authenticate them. Although this doesn't go to the truth of the content of the article itself, the article can be introduced to show that the statement was published without the necessity of dragging the reporter or the publisher in to say, "Yes, I wrote that."

One other pitfall of testifying is that litigants will sometimes attempt to trade on the credibility of the newspaper if their credibility is suspect. A litigant should stand on her own credibility and not attempt to use the good reputation of the newspaper to bolster her position.

Subpoenas can be disruptive. You should have a specific policy on subpoenas and then stick to it.

Confidential Sources

Confidential sources pose special problems. Although many courts will not compel you to reveal the identity of a confidential source or the full content of your conversation, you also do not have absolute freedom to name sources to whom you have promised anonymity in a story, absent a subpoena. In a 1991 Minnesota case the U.S. Supreme Court ruled that two newspapers could be sued for violating their reporter's promise that a source, Dan Cohen, associated with one candidate's gubernatorial campaign, would not be named in connection with a newspaper story. After investigating information that Cohen provided about public court records concerning an opponent in the 1982 governor's race the two newspapers, The St. Paul pioneer Press Dispatch and the Minneapolis Star and Tribune decided to name Cohen as the source of the documents. He was fired from his campaign post the day the stories appeared. He sued alleging breach of contract and fraudulent misrepresentation. When the case was remanded to the Minnesota Supreme Court it held that Cohen was entitled to $200,000 in damages.[4]

In 1996 a Michigan State University scholar Hugh J. Martin reviewed 22 First Amendment cases which had cited **Cohen v Cowles Media Co., 19 Med. L. Rptr. 1858; 479 NW2d 387 (1992)** and concluded the cases showed "courts have upheld damage awards when journalists break promises of confidentiality to victims of HIV and sexual abuse." However, he observed that it apparently "does not allow enforcement of confidentiality if the identity of a source already is public or if the source failed to make the conditions of the promise clear." And he concluded that "Cohen may have implications for cases involving undercover reporting techniques."[5]

As a reporter you should also remember that most news organizations believe that your sources belong to them so before you casually offer anonymity to a source, ask yourself "is this really necessary?" In addition you should check with your supervisors on the matter. Otherwise if you decide to protect your source from your supervisor you may find yourself paying for your own attorney and out of work.

Broadcaster Immunity

Under the Federal Communications Commission's Equal Time Rules a broadcaster is immune from liability resulting from a political candidate's remarks when that person is exercising his or her rights to use the station facilities. Since the broadcaster may not censor the comments the courts do not hold them accountable for their content.

Subpoenas

If you cover or edit crime and government stories or disasters such as fires, auto accidents and the like, you are going to be occasionally served with a subpoena to appear at a deposition or to appear in Court to testify. Do not panic when the process server turns up at your 6 a.m. racquetball match. Just accept the papers and immediately contact your supervisor, who will take care of contacting your attorney. You have not done anything wrong nor have you committed a crime. It merely means that you have something that the government or the lawyers want and your news organization has to decide whether or not it wants you to give it to them.

There is no absolute privilege of reporters to disobey a subpoena. You should never ignore a subpoena. But you should not provide any information in response to a subpoena without first consulting with your editor. News media attorneys were able to quash subpoenas more than 70 percent of the time, according to one study by The Reporters Committee for Freedom of the Press, but they also reported several instances in which law enforcement authorities searched newsrooms looking for information and two 1993 cases where reporters were jailed for failing to comply with subpoenas. [6]

News organizations take a dim view of subpoenas in most circumstances, especially if they involve information obtained from confidential or protected sources. Routine subpoenas of reporters interferes with news gathering. Not only does the reporter spend valuable time cooling her heels in a lawyer's office or a court room, but sources are more reticent if they believe the reporter will routinely hand their statements over to police. Then there is the issue of confidential sources who have an expectation of confidentiality. But there are exceptions, so get the subpoena into the hands of your supervisor and the attorneys for the news organization.

A subpoena may be quashed (that means voided by a court), withdrawn or modified. Almost every subpoena can be narrowed or limited in scope. However, the most important thing is to give out no information voluntarily in response to a subpoena until your response has been determined by your news organization. A reporter is not an agent of the government. Voluntarily giving information to the government especially pursuant to a subpoena jeopardizes your ability to resist other subpoenas. Although information is often shared in the investigative stage of a story, a formal subpoena is a horse of a different color.

There are several factors to be taken into account when formulating your response to a subpoena.

- **Is this subpoena in a criminal matter (more difficult to oppose) or a civil matter?**
- **Does this subpoena ask for confirmation of published information or unpublished information?**
- **Does this subpoena ask for information obtained from a source who had an expectation of confidentiality?**
- **Does this subpoena ask for information obtained from a source to whom you promised confidentiality?**
- **Does this subpoena ask for information which the newspaper routinely provides such as photographs for a fee?**

It is also important to be consistent in opposing subpoenas. If you routinely provide information requested in subpoenas without objection a court will not be sympathetic to your protest when you do not want to provide the information

You must also draw a distinction between confidential sources and non-confidential sources. The courts are usually willing to protect confidential sources more than non-confidential ones.

The best defense is a good offense. Your news organization should have a policy on responding to subpoenas before the reporters receive one. That policy should not be in writing unless you want it subpoenaed. But you should discuss the underlying issues of the impact of divulging information on news gathering, the duty of reporters, if any, to provide police assistance, the policy on promising confidentiality to sources and who is in charge of making the determinations.

In helping you formulate a policy the following discussion of the law will be useful.

Subpoenas To Testify And Provide Documents

Under the First Amendment journalists possess a qualified privilege to refuse to disclose their confidential and non-confidential sources and background information. **Branzburg v Hayes, 408 US 665; 92 S Ct 2646; 33 L Ed 2d 626 (1972).** This "newswriters' privilege" has been widely recognized by the federal and state courts as essential to the integrity of the news gathering process guaranteed under the First Amendment:

> **The autonomy of the press would be jeopardized if resort to its resource materials, by litigants seeking to utilize the news gathering efforts of journalists for their private purposes, were routinely permitted. . . . Moreover, because journalists typically gather information about accidents, crimes, and other matters of special interest that often give rise to litigation, attempts to obtain evidence by subjecting the press to discovery as a nonparty would be widespread if not restricted. The practical burdens on time and resources, as well as the consequent diversion of journalistic effort and disruption of news gathering activity, would be particularly inimical to the vigor of a free press. O'Neill v Oakgrove Construction Inc, 71 NY2d 521, 526; 523 NE2d 277, 279 (1988) (citations omitted).**

Another case concluded "the compelled disclosure of a reporter's resource materials can constitute a significant intrusion into the news gathering and editorial processes. . .(and) may substantially undercut the public policy favoring the free flow of information to the public that is the foundation for the privilege," **United States v Cuthbertson, 630 F2d 139; 147 (CA 3, 1980), cert den, 449 US 1126 (1981).**

Generally speaking a journalist can be compelled to disclose information regarding his or her sources and background information only where the party seeking disclosure demonstrates that the materials sought are:

1. **Highly material.**
2. **Critical to its claims.**
3. **Unavailable from any other source.**

The Michigan Court of Appeals has expressly adopted the newswriter's privilege to bar the disclosure of a reporter's confidential sources absent a showing that the requested information "goes to the heart of the litigant's case" and is unavailable by any other means. **King v Photo Marketing Association International**, 120 Mich App 527; 327 NW2d 515, 517-518 (1982).

Importantly, several state and federal courts have ruled that the newswriter's privilege precludes a litigant using the compelled testimony of a reporter to impeach the credibility of a witness who denies the accuracy of published quotations attributed to him. [7]

A Michigan case illustrates the importance of having a well thought out policy. In **Marketos v American Employers Insurance Company, 185 Mich App 179; 460 NW2d 272 (1990)**, the Court required the newspaper to provide the defendant with various unpublished, non-confidential photographs of a fire scene. But the reason the Court was unsympathetic was that until just before the subpoena was served the newspaper had a policy of selling its photos, published and unpublished, for a nominal amount. Furthermore, it is clear that it is important to establish by affidavits or otherwise that the subpoena imposed a substantial administrative burden upon the news organization. Therefore a news organization should consider the burden of a subpoena and adopt a policy with regard to responding that is consistent.

Grand Jury Subpoenas

A subpoena from a state grand jury must meet the above standards. The Branzburg qualified privilege has been codified in the grand jury statute. Although it is applicable only to grand jury proceedings it is useful to point out to a judge that grand juries are so limited. Surely if a grand jury can't force a journalist to testify except under specified circumstances, then a similar standard should be applied in other subpoena situations.

Alternatives To Responding

Many subpoenas are quashed or withdrawn when a reporter signs an affidavit that the material that appeared in the newspaper or on the air is accurate and was produced by the reporter.

A news organization can seek a protective order to limit the subpoena. Most newspapers oppose efforts to obtain their reporters' notes on the basis that criminal or civil investigators should gather their own information. A reporter is not an agent of the government. There are exceptions when a court orders you to turn over material. At that point follow the advice your counsel unless you want to spend some time in jail for contempt.

Newsroom Searches

Search warrants are another matter. Search warrants are issued by police upon approval of a judge or magistrate. They are used as part of an investigation before charges are issued. Do not encourage or agree to a search warrant. Search warrants of newsrooms are not permitted except in certain special circumstances.

Ignorance of the law is no excuse, according to the old admonition. But no one has figured out what to say when the judge, the assistant prosecutor, the police officer, the editor and the reporter are all unaware of the law.

In September 1990 a reporter for the Macomb Daily, a 45,000 circulation newspaper operating in Mt. Clemens, Michigan, about 25 miles north of Detroit, had interviewed the mother of a victim in a drive-by shooting, one of those where the assailant doesn't have the courtesy to stop and introduce himself. The witness then refused to talk about some of the same things reported in the paper to police officers investigating the crime. So detectives asked the reporter if she would let them review her notes because they felt there were some discrepancies in the woman's account. When the reporter checked with her editors they said, no. If you want the reporter's notes you can subpoena them and we'll see you in court.

The Warren police met with a Macomb County assistant prosecuting attorney and asked for a search warrant on Sept. 26. The warrant was rejected by District Court Judge Thomas Kennedy as being too broad since it asked for a search of the Macomb Daily building which included the offices of attorneys and medical professionals.

The next day the officers reinterviewed the witness and were told by the witness that the reporter had confused her statements with someone else.

On Friday, Sept. 28 the investigators drafted a second search warrant and presented it to another District Judge, who approved it.

On Saturday morning when only a few employees were present two detectives from Warren appeared at The Macomb Daily offices in Mount Clemens with a search warrant for the notes. The reporter helped them get into the building by pressing a buzzer that unlocked a rear door, showed them where the notes were, watched them confiscate them and then phoned her managing editor alleging she was surprised by the invasion and note confiscation. The Managing Editor naturally raised a fuss and called the Editor, who was coincidentally nearby touring the County Jail with his Indian Guides unit.

The editor called the County Prosecutor, the newspaper's attorneys and other prominent newspaper attorneys. The Detroit media jumped on the story and reported it as did television and national media outlets. All agreed that the seizure should never have occurred , but it was a day or so before the correct federal statue was located. On Monday the notes were recovered and the police department admitted they had worked with the reporter to execute the search warrant when senior managers wouldn't be present. They apologized and the reporter was disciplined.

The federal statute called the First Amendment Privacy Protection Act was passed after a 1978 U.S. Supreme Court decision upholding the legality of a police raid on the news room of Stanford University's Stanford Daily and it bars the seizure of a journalist's notes except under extraordinary conditions.

In case you are ever confronted with such a moment the law states:

Notwithstanding any other law, it shall be unlawful for a government officer or employee, in connection with the investigation or prosecution of a criminal offense, to search for or seize any work product materials possessed by a person reasonably believed to have a purpose to disseminate to the public a newspaper, books broadcast or other similar form of publication, in or affecting interstate or foreign commerce. . . . 29 USC 2000 aa.

There are a couple of exceptions. If the investigators believe the person possessing the materials has committed or is committing a criminal offense to which the materials relate or if there is reason to believe the seizure is necessary to prevent bodily injury to a human being.

The correct course for the officers would have been to produce a subpoena and allow The Macomb Daily attorneys an opportunity to submit an affidavit setting forth the basis for any contention that the materials sought were not subject to seizure.

In this case the Warren press release admitted: "The progress of the homicide investigation does not rely solely on the information contained within this reporter's notebook. This was just one questionable area that officers were trying to clear up."

Your first step in such a case is to contact your editor, your publisher and your attorney and to advise such officers that there are legal penalties for improperly executing such a search warrant. Naturally if the officers ignore those admonitions you should cooperate and document with witnesses and photograph their activities while in your office.

1. "The First Amendment and the Fourth Estate, the Law of Mass Media" 6th edition, by T. Barton Carter, Marc A. Franklin and Jay B. Wright, pp. 520-535.

2. The Newsman's Privilege: An Empirical Study, by Vince Blasi, 70 Michigan Law Review 229, 231-232, 284 (1971) reprinted in "The First Amendment and the Fourth Estate, pp. 519-520, The Foundation Press, N.Y. 1994.

3. Survey of Michigan Libel Law, with developments reported through Aug. 1, 1996, by John J. Ronayne and Bronson Murray, p. 11.

4. The First Amendment and the Fourth Estate, The Law of Mass Media, 6th ed., by Carter, Franklin and Wright, pp. 550-557.

5. American Educators in Journalism and Mass Communications (AEJMC) News , July 1996, pg. 20.

6. New York Times, Mar. 27, 1995 C6.

7. United States v Hendron, 820 F.Supp 715; 21 Med. L. Rptr. 1506, (EDNY. 1993) (defendant's subpoena to reporter quashed where he "failed to make the clear and specific showing that the (materials) are necessary or critical to the maintenance of the defense); United States v Paez, 13 Med. L. Rptr. 1973, (SD Fla, 1987) (criminal defendants failed to show that reporter's testimony to be used for impeachment purposes was central to their defense, admissible and unavailable from any other source); Florida v Kangus, 8 Med. L. Rptr. 2045 (bar attempt to compel testimony of reporter to impeach State Attorney with prior statements).

Chapter 4

Reporting the Courts Check List

1. Trials must be open to the public except under extreme circumstances.

2. All hearings in a courtroom including preliminary examinations are ordinarily open to the public. Special statutes exist for the closure of some hearings. See Michigan Compiled Laws 766.9 for closure of preliminary exams.

3. You should make friends with the court scheduling clerk. This person can be a great source and help.

4. In general files of the court are open to the public and that right to inspect them is set forth in the Michigan Court Rules.

5. If you think there is a chance a judge will issue an order to close a court room you should check with your editor and your editor should check with your attorney in advance.

6. If a judges orders a hearing closed unexpectedly you should ask permission to read the following statement to the court:

> **"Your Honor, may it please Court. My name is (*insert name*) from the (*insert newspaper's name*). Sir or Madam, I respectfully request permission to address the Court on the sole issue of closing the Courtroom. I understand under MCR 8.116 that the news organization has standing to raise this matter with the Court. I would appreciate having the opportunity to have our attorney come to the court house to discuss the closure of the court room."**

7. If requested, the court is required to schedule a hearing on the issue of closing the court. Michigan Court Rule 8.116. The test for closing any hearing is similar to the one for closing Preliminary Examinations found at Michigan Compiled Laws 766.9. If the judge proceeds request respectfully that he state on the record the reasons and evidence to support closing the hearing.

8. Always be respectful in court and dress appropriately.

9. Know the court rules for the courts you are covering: there are local rules.

10. If a judge feels it will hamper the fair administration of a trial or he or she feels court rules have been violated the judge can exclude coverage of part or all of a proceeding. These rulings are subject to appeal.

11. Since 1989 cameras and video equipment have been allowed in Michigan court rooms. You should make the request in writing to the court clerk at least three business days before the proceeding is scheduled to begin. These rulings are not subject to appeal.

Chapter 4

Reporting the Courts

Under the U.S. system of government there is a dual court system. There is a state trial court and a federal trial court, a Michigan Court of Appeals and Federal Courts of Appeals and a Michigan Supreme Court (seven black robes) and a U.S. Supreme Court (nine black robes).

One of the most helpful tools your news organization should own for keeping the courts in order is the Michigan State Bar Journal. It is $35 and can be purchased from the State Bar of Michigan located at 306 Townsend St., Lansing, MI 4893. It contains lists, names, addresses and telephone numbers of all the federal courts affecting Michigan and of all Michigan courts, attorneys, state agencies and some federal agencies and many more people, places and things.

Michigan Courts

In Michigan trial courts are called Circuit Courts (for claims over $10,000) and District Courts (for claims under $10,000). They are divided into 57 circuits and 98 districts.

District Courts handle civil suits under $10,000, landlord/tenant matters including evictions; land contract forfeitures; traffic violations; misdemeanors; and arraignments for all crimes. More than one District Court may feed cases into a Circuit Court. District Courts are generally divided by communities; Circuit Courts are determined by county and may include more than one.

Small Claims is a division of District Court and does not allow lawyers to represent litigants on claims of $1,750 or less.

Probate Court handles probate and estate matters and mentally incompetent and physically incompetent persons. Hearings in probate court are open unless the court determines that openness would jeopardize the rights of a party.

The new Family Division of the Circuit Court handles divorce, adoption, custody, paternity and child support, abuse and neglect, juvenile proceedings, personal protection orders, and name changes. While most newspapers do not print the names of juveniles except in special circumstances it is not against the law to print them. It is a matter of judgment.

State Appellate Courts

The Michigan Court of Appeals is divided into three divisions. Cases appealed from Wayne go to the First Division, Oakland to the Second. Details of where your county's appeals go is included in the State Bar Journal.

Courts of Appeal hold sessions in Detroit, Lansing, Grand Rapids and Marquette. Three judges hear oral arguments on cases.

The Clerk's office of the Michigan Court of Appeals is one of the most professional staffs you will ever meet. They are polite, courteous and helpful. Do not abuse them and you will be rewarded.

The Michigan Supreme Court is the court of last resort in Michigan. While litigants may appeal to the Michigan Court of Appeals as a matter of right, they must ask the Supreme Court for leave to appeal. This request is made by filing an Application for Leave to Appeal with the Michigan Supreme Court. Generally, only a small percentage of cases are taken for consideration by the Michigan Supreme Court each year.

Federal Courts

Federal trial courts are called District Courts. Federal courts have jurisdiction of cases between citizens of different states and for matters specifically determined by federal statute. They also have jurisdiction of federal crimes such as robbery of federally insured banks.

Michigan has an Eastern District and a Western District. The Eastern District holds court at Detroit, Flint and Bay City. The Western District holds court at Grand Rapids, Kalamazoo and Marquette.

Appeals from district courts go to the Circuit Courts of Appeal . Michigan is in the Sixth Circuit along with Ohio, Indiana, Wisconsin, Kentucky and Tennessee. The Sixth Circuit meets in Cincinnati.

The U.S. Supreme Court considers appeals from the federal circuits courts of appeal and state courts of appeal. In order to appeal to the U.S. Supreme Court, one must obtain permission. The request for permission is called a Writ of Certiorari. If the "petition for cert" as it is referred to is granted, full fledge briefs are filed with the Court and arguments held before all nine justices in Washington, D.C.

Court Clerks

Every court has a court clerk. It may be the County Clerk in small counties. In large counties it is a separate position called the Circuit Court Clerk. That clerk and his staff are in charge of the administrative functions of the Court and of the file room. The Clerk of the Court can be helpful in terms of reviewing files and knowing dockets and letting you know what cases may be particularly interesting.

Each judge also has assistants sometimes called a deputy clerk. These individuals set schedules and are a fountain of information.

Make friends with scheduling clerks. Scheduling clerks rule the court world. Many scheduling clerks are law students, but many are permanent positions.

Many judges in large counties and all federal judges have law clerks. They are usually recent law graduates. They are knowledgeable about the law and help you gain access to the judge.

Law clerks and judges come and go. Scheduling clerks seem to stay forever. They have tenure; are not elected and most are civil servants. They get reassigned to the new judges. Accord them respect and your days as a court beat reporter will be easier.

Court Reporter

Each judge has a court reporter to take down the words of courtroom proceedings. The court reporter is a busy person. A court reporter does not make a transcript of everything that happens in the courtroom. A court reporter does not transcribe what occurs unless someone orders a transcript and pays for it. Transcripts are expensive and time consuming to prepare. In most cases your company will not want to pay for an entire transcript. However, the attorneys for both sides frequently buy them and if they feel it is in their interest they will let you look at them. Take good notes or make a request to have a tape recorder in the courtroom.

Court Files

Court files are kept in the file room of the Clerk's office. They are open for inspection subject to the rules of that particular court. Files are in the judge's chamber when the judge is hearing a case or working on the case. They are still accessible if you ask. **Michigan Court Rule 8.105** provides for access to files except as limited by order of the court or statute.

Court Rules

The rules of the court are a useful tool for a courts reporter. There are both Michigan Court Rules and Federal Court Rules. These rules describe the time lines for a lawsuit, the kinds of motions that may be filed and the kinds of documents which need to be filed.

Michigan Court Rules discuss all of the various courts and proceedings in chapters. Federal Court rule on the other hand are divided up into Civil Rules, Criminal Procedure, Appellate Rules, etc. All of these court rules will assist you in understanding the lingo of the justice system and the order in which things will proceed.

Civil Cases

Civil cases commence through the filing of a complaint. Defendants then have an opportunity to file an answer or to file a motion to dismiss sometimes called a motion for summary judgment or summary disposition. During the course of the litigation the parties can engage in discovery. Discovery covers a lot of activities which allow a party to place the other party under oath for deposition upon oral examination, to respond to written questions, to produce documents, to allow examination of property and the testing of the property. These results are generally not in the court file unless they are filed in support of a motion.

Open Courts

Openness in government is embodied in the Michigan Constitution of 1963 as well as in Michigan statutes and Court rules. **MCL 600.1420** provides in part that: "The sittings of every court within this state shall be public. . ." **MCR 8.116** authorizes any person to object to an order of closure of a court proceeding. Check **Appendix 3** for a detailed account of what to say if a Judge should order a court closed.

Likewise the Court rules recognize that in general files of the Court are also open to the public. **MCR 8.105** provides that "unless access to a file is restricted by statue, court rule, or a suppression order, any person may inspect pleadings and other papers in the clerk's office and may obtain copies. . ."

Hearings

This raises the issue of when court proceedings and files may be closed to the public. Criminal proceedings have generated legislation and case law as to when judicial hearings may be closed.

In the landmark case of **Press-Enterprise** v **Riverside County Superior Court, 478 US 1; 106 S Ct 2735; 92 L Ed 2d (1986)**, a case known as *Press Enterprise II*, (to be distinguished from a prior case involving the same newspaper and the importance of open jury selection), the U.S. Supreme Court again set forth the test for closing criminal proceedings. It ruled a preliminary examination should have been open to the public, reiterating the test which the Court developed over 20 years.

In considering whether a hearing should be open or closed the Court said that it must first determine whether or not the hearing has traditionally been open to the public.

If the hearing has traditionally been an open hearing, the court must balance the right of the public to an open hearing against the rights being asserted in favor of closing it. In reviewing the answer to the second part of the test the Court must make the following analysis at a hearing at which the press is allowed to appear and argue the matter.:

A. After a hearing at which the court can evaluate the competing interests, and determine which right should prevail.

B. If the Court determines that closure is necessary, the Court must state the specific reason for closure on the record.

C. And must tailor the closure as narrowly as possibly so as not to infringe any more than is necessary on the public right to know.

In considering the closure of a preliminary examination the high court said this:

1. Because of its extensive scope, the preliminary hearing is often the final and most important in the criminal proceeding. As the California Supreme Court stated in **San Jose Mercury-News v Municipal Court**, 30 Cal.3d 498; 638 P.2d 655; 179 Cal.Rptr 772 (1982). the preliminary hearing in many cases provides "the sole occasion for public observation of the criminal justice system

2. "The absence of a jury, long recognized as "An inestimable safeguard against the corrupt or overzealous prosecutor and against the compliant, biased or eccentric judge," makes the importance of public access to a preliminary hearing even more significant.

3. "Criminal acts, especially certain violent crimes, provoke public concern, outrage, and hostility, "When the public is aware that the law is being enforced and the criminal justice system is functioning, an outlet is provided for these understandable reactions and emotions"

4. And from Press Enterprise II quoting from Press Enterprise I: The value of openness lies in the fact that people not actually attending trials can have confidence that standards of fairness are being observed; the sure knowledge that anyone is free to attend gives assurance that established procedures are being followed and that deviations will become known. Openness thus enhances both the basic fairness of the criminal trial and the appearance of fairness so essential to public confidence in the system.

5. Lastly the Court indicated that in order to settle rights in conflict when closing is requested, a hearing must be held where "specific findings are made demonstrating that first, there is a substantial probability that the defendant's right to a fair trial will be prejudiced by publicity that closure would prevent and, second, reasonable alternatives closure cannot adequately protect defendant's fair trial rights."

Similarly in the case of **Globe Newspaper** v **Superior Court**, 457 US 596; 102 S Ct 2613 (1982), the United States Supreme Court said that a criminal hearing could not be closed to protect juvenile witnesses without determining on a case by case basis whether closure is necessary to protect the welfare of a minor victim. The court indicated that the court must weigh various factors to determine the proper result. The court rejected the suggestion of the Commonwealth of Massachusetts that closure would encourage victims to come forward since there was no evidence to support such an assertion.

This line of cases was cited by the Michigan Court of Appeals in the case of **Booth Newspapers, Inc** v **12th District Judge**, 172 Mich App 688; 432 NW2d 400 (1988) in holding that **MCL 750.520k** was unconstitutional under Press Enterprise II. This statute allowed courts to seal files on criminal sexual conduct charges up to the time of arraignment. This statute is no longer valid. Instead the court must make the foregoing analysis.

The preliminary exam itself must now be open unless it meets the standards of Press-Enterprise II. The Michigan legislature has amended the statute on preliminary examinations to set forth the same test used by the U.S. Supreme Court. See **MCL 766.9**. That statute mandates that a court only close the preliminary exam when:

A. **The magistrate or judge determines that the need for protection of a victim, a witness or the defendant outweighs the public's right to access.**

B. **The denial of access to the examination is narrowly tailored to accommodate the interest being protected.**

C. **The magistrate or judge states on the record the specific reasons for his or her decision to close the examination.**

The statute lists factors to be considered in closing a trial for the benefit of witnesses or victims and also things to be considered if the defendant fears an open hearing will impair his right of fair trial.

Thus, the U.S. Supreme Court and the Michigan Courts recognize that closure of criminal proceedings is only to be considered in situation meeting the standard set forth above.

Trials

Generally trials cannot be closed. A judge may close portions of a trial in the event of extraordinary circumstances but the same rules apply. There must be a hearing and the Court must find an interest as important as the First Amendment right of access and must use the least restrictive means possible to preserve the important interest.

Documents

The same basic principles apply to documents as well. The Michigan Court Rules provide that files shall be open unless closed by order of the Court. **MCL 8.105**. In **Nixon** v **Warner Communications**, 435 US 589; 98 S Ct 1306; 55 L Ed 2d 570 (1978), the Supreme Court recognized that the press and the public have a common law right of access to judicial records.

In **Capital Cities Broadcasting Corporation** v **Tenth District Judge**, 91 Mich App 655; 283 NW2d 779 (1979), the Michigan Court of Appeals stated it this way:

> **Freedom of the press and the public nature of court documents require a hearing, open to all interested parties, before inspection of public court documents may be denied. The purpose of this hearing is to explore the constitutional and statutory validity of any proffered justifications for non-inspection and to determine whether any alternative and less restrictive mechanism than complete suppression exist. Id. p. 657**

MCR 8.105 (D) now sets forth the requirements for sealing of Court records. As in closed judicial proceedings the court must make a finding of good cause to seal the records and must be sure there is no less restrictive means to adequately and effectively protect the specific interest served.

The sealing of Court records is deemed so significant that whenever the courts grants a motion to seal a court record, the court must forward a copy of the order to the Michigan Clerk of the supreme Court and to the State Court Administrator.

Standing

Michigan Court Rules provide standing to any person to challenge the closure of Court hearings and files. Thus **MCR 8.116** states that any person may file a motion to set aside the order or object to a proposed order of closure.

Likewise **MCR 8.105 (D) (6)** provides that any person may file a motion to set aside an order that seals a record or object to the entry of such an order.

Cameras in the Courtroom

A 1989 administrative order altered the Michigan Code of Judicial Conduct and allows cameras, tape recorders and other electronic equipment into courtrooms under certain restrictions.

In order to film or electronically report on court proceedings you must make a request in writing to the clerk at least three business days before the proceeding is scheduled to begin. Although a judge at his or her discretion can waive this time period. The Court must notify the parties to the proceeding and they can object to such coverage.

A judge may terminate, suspend, limit or exclude film or electronic media coverage at any time upon a finding, made on the record, that fair administration of justice requires such action or that other court rules have been violated. The judge has broad discretion to exclude coverage of certain witnesses such as sex crime victims or their families, informants, undercover agents and relocated witnesses.

Film or electronic media coverage of the jury selection process or the jurors is not permitted and audio or video recording of conferences between attorneys, clients, and judges in the court room are not allowed.

No more than two still cameras, two television cameras and one tape recording are allowed in a courtroom at one time. The Court may also reduce that number. The media are responsible for making their own pool arrangements under such circumstances. If they can't work it out there is no coverage and there are no appeals to a higher court on such arrangements.

That doesn't mean the trial court can limit physical access of reporters to the courtroom without fear of an appeal. It just means there is no appeal on arrangements for electronic or film coverage.

The media are responsible for making sure that the equipment is quiet, that their actions in operating the equipment is unobtrusive and it is placed where the judge has ordered. A copy of the rules, which are fairly specific, can be found in Appendix Four.

Remember, this rule does not affect the right of reporters to observe the proceedings. Any order limiting your ability to observe proceedings is subject to appeal and must meet the requirements of the Court Rules and the Constitution.

Conclusion

Whether a court is considering the suppression of a court file or of a court hearing, it is required by the U.S. Supreme Court, Michigan Statutes, court rules, and Michigan case law to do the following:

1. **Hold a hearing on the issue of closure.**

2. **Balance the right of access against the right asserted for closure, recognizing that closure is to be ordered only when the court finds an overriding interest based on specific findings that closure is essential to preserving a higher value.**

3. **If the court finds an overriding interest, the Court must state the reasons for closure on the record.**

4. **If the court finds closure is appropriate, fashion the least restrictive means of protecting the rights asserted for closure.**

In making the determination on closure, the Court must keep in mind the statement of the Supreme Court in the Press-Enterprise cases, I and II:

> **Openness in criminal trials, including the selection of jurors, "enhances both the basic fairness of the criminal trial and the appearance of fairness so essential to public confidence in the system."**

Chapter 5

Reporting on Government And Government Agencies - Check List:

1. Get the document to support any claim you make.

2. Don't juice, goose or attempt to sharpen the language in a story that is potentially libelous. Famous New York Times Pulitzer winner Harrison Salisbury said there aren't any boring stories, only boring reporters. But it is safer to be a little boring with difficult material.

3. Avoid injecting any comment or opinion traceable to the news staff.

4. Be fair in your report. Get comment from all sides or make an honest effort to do so. The Detroit News once reported a local police chief was unavailable for comment and readers pointed out the News had run the man's obituary a few days earlier.

5. Make sure the charge you say a person is convicted of is exactly that charge.

6. Civil complaints should be handled more carefully still. Get both sides and be wary of frivolous charges or charges that could destroy a person's reputation.

7. Make sure a complaint has been filed and served. Don't just accept a copy from a plaintiff's attorney who delivers it to your office.

8. Always get comment from the other side if someone provides you with a deposition. Make sure you have the entire deposition.

9. Press releases, governmental studies and statistical compilations drawn from them may be reported without liability. If it seems odd make sure it is a legitimate document.

10. A police log is a running summary of the first impressions of officers on a given day. It is often inaccurate and should contain a reporter warning: "This log could be harmful to your legal costs."

11. Follow this rule: "When in doubt, leave it out."

12. Make sure headlines are accurate in every detail.

Chapter 5

Reporting on Government and Public Agencies.

There is lots of high sounding rhetoric about what the role of the press is in America and Michigan. But let's face it up front. Many of the powers that be, including the framers of the Constitution and the Bill of Rights and most Michigan lawmakers, judges, legislators, etc. saw us, and see us, as a necessary evil; junkyard dogs which serve a useful purpose in arousing the citizenry when danger is at hand, but not the kind of creatures you would invite into your home to share your hearth.

Many governmental officials accept the principle of an unfettered press serving as the watchdog of the masses, they just don't want the damned dog barking at them.
So we have a love-hate relationship that will continue to be played out in the courts and newspaper pages of the land. And as a newspaper editor or reporter you better hope your company has deep pockets when it comes to defending itself against an aggrieved citizen. Your job is to make sure you are right. Being right doesn't insulate you from being sued, but it does make your attorney feel a lot better when she gets to court.

Here are three quick rules to help you in covering government stories since most of what we write are government stories. police, fire, crime, city councils, zoning boards and mosquito control districts are all under the heading.

1. **Get documentation.**
2. **Get documentation.**
3. **Get documentation.**

It is not documented if the sheriff stops you outside the beauty parlor and slips you some quick and dirty gossip about his primary opponent's sexual persuasions. It is not documented if the Mayor tells you that the new civic center can't be built because John Tightwad is committing highway robbery with his price on the land.

That doesn't mean you can't quote those individuals. It just means you better have more to go on before you besmirch the reputation of some fellow who has never been convicted of being a robber baron. Just because he walks like a robber baron, talks like a robber baron, and looks like a robber baron does not make it so.

As Jack Webb used to say in his Joe Friday Dragnet television role:

"Just the facts, ma'am. Just the facts." Facts in government stories are government records, filings, pleadings, reports, sworn affidavits, etc. You will make your friendly libel attorney happy if you can provide such items to back up your grand expose. And more importantly you will make your publisher happy too.

Under the Michigan Freedom of Information Act whether you are a private citizen or a reporter you should have reasonable access to most of this stuff at a fair charge for copying. That is dealt with in Chapter 6.

The special privilege of the news media in this country traces to the phrase the Founding Fathers put in the first amendment to the Constitution: Congress shall make no law abridging the freedom of the press.

Libel law recognizes the importance of the media in reporting on government so you can print, publish or broadcast official proceedings without fear of liability.

That still doesn't mean you can't be sued if you include defamatory statements made during a meeting by the City Council President in your story. If the governmental body makes the defamatory statements it is one thing, if an individual makes them it may be another.

For example if the City Council President said Joe Smith, who is applying for a liquor license is a known pervert and you simply quoted that without checking the facts you and your publication would be at risk. It might not be true. You might damage Smith's ability to do business in the community.

Here is what the Michigan libel statute, **MCL 600.2911** provides:

> **Damages shall not be awarded in a libel action for the publication or broadcast of a fair and true report of:**
>
> **1. matters of public record.**
> **2. a public and official proceeding.**
> **3. a governmental notice, announcement, written or recorded report or record generally available to the public.**
> **4. an act or action of a public body.**
> **5. the heading of a report which is a fair and true.**

Now, here's a catch you have to watch:

> **This privilege shall not apply to a libel which is contained in a matter added by a person concerned in the publication or contained in the report of anything said or done at the time and place of the public and official proceeding or governmental notice.**

We've already dealt with your not simply repeating libelous remarks by a city official. The other part of the catch is you editors out there. Don't juice, goose or boost a story to make it more readable if you are dealing with potentially libelous material. It is a swamp on which you do not want to tread. "There are no boring stories only boring reporters," said New York Times Pulitzer winner Harrison Salisbury. Salisbury had returned from a European assignment as a young star and the desk palmed off a Sulzberger favorite trash collection story on him to bring him down a peg or two. So he spent several months on the subject and won a prize for his efforts. James Steele, Pulitzer prize winner for the Philadelphia Inquirer, who, with his reporting partner Don Bartlett, has written some of the most complex stories about our society in readable English, extends that to say "there are a lot of boring reporters and editors." But before editors get creative they should talk to reporters. Smoothing out that complicated statement, summary or quote is frequently an invitation to hear the chac(c)hing of your libel attorney's cash register.

Words like fraud, theft, forge, steal, filch, phony, fake, cheat all have two things in common. They fit easily into headlines and they give your attorney sweaty palms.

Fair and True Report

Most lawsuits come from the caveat that your reporting should be "fair and true." Your attorney will tell you that once you move beyond the document to comment you have stepped out on the slippery slope. You are caught in the dilemma of being Harrison Salisbury's "boring reporter" or trying to make some sense out of the gobbledegook that bureaucrats, public officials and attorneys pass over for English.

Remember, every libel plaintiff (that's the fellow complaining) believes your report has been unfair. And frequently at the trial court level juries agree with them. So Rule Number Four is after you get the document make sure you are fair in how you report it. In simpler times there were just facts and falsehoods. Now days we have "true facts," "false facts," partial facts," "presumed facts," "irrelevant facts" and "unknown facts." As an attorney in the Tom Cruise, Demi Moore, Jack Nicholson movie, "A Few Good Men" observed, the "liar, liar pants are on fire," defense doesn't suffice anymore.

David Lawrence, one-time Publisher of The Detroit Free Press and now doing similar duty at The Miami Herald, once wrote "the search for truth is an elusive pursuit." Right.

One of the most famous libel cases in Michigan in the 1980's eventually caused the State Legislature to try to re-define what is a public document. **Rouch v Enquirer & News of Battle Creek, 440 Mich 238; 487 NW2d 205 (1992).**

Until David Rouch sued The Battle Creek Enquirer for libel reporters, editors and attorneys assumed that arrest and police reports were official proceedings and thus protected. But when the Jurists got their hands on the case as it wound its way up through the legal system they opined that the newspaper might have legally used the name of the person arrested and not the charge or they might have used the charge, but not the name of the person arrested.

That could have made for some interesting, but strange newspaper stories. John Doe was arrested on unspecified charges by police today or an unidentified business leader was charged in a series of slayings. What the justices said was that statutory protection extended to judicial proceedings and perhaps administrative proceedings, but not police incident reports or police conduct.

In response the legislature adopted this broad definition of "the document as a government notice, announcement, written or recorded report or record generally available to the public and all matters of public record and records of public and official proceedings.

Matters of Public Record

Police reports in most instances are a matter of public record. The law makes exceptions for information that could endanger a witness or victim or hamper an ongoing police investigation. One key case in support of your position with the local Chief of Police is **The Evening News Association vs. City of Troy**. In this case a resident had hidden himself in his van to try to apprehend some vandals. Two Troy officers got a report that something suspicious was happening at the van and when they arrived they saw movement in the vehicle and shot and killed the resident. Troy police refused to release the identities of the officers. Reasoning that if anyone else had shot someone under similar circumstances the name would have been made public, the Detroit News went to court and asked for them. At each level of the Michigan court system the judges advised Troy that the police officers were due no special protection or privilege. Ultimately after several years the Michigan Supreme Court confirmed that position and ordered Troy to pay The Detroit News more than $40,000 in legal fees.

You will find that case summarized in an Appendix. If you are having trouble getting information from your police department make copies of it and give them to the Chief and the desk sergeant. It will give them something to think about.

That is not to say that you should be part of the full employment for attorneys brigade and sue every time you don't get what you want. For example, after an Albion police officer shot himself in the foot during pistol practice, the department refused to identify him because of the potential embarrassment. The Jackson Citizen Patriot didn't print the story, according to a reporter, because they couldn't confirm it with the police report document.

Common sense would suggest that you show them the summary of the Troy case and file a freedom of information request. Then a little good legwork among the officers in a department Albion's size would confirm which officer was limping around, on medical leave, or otherwise among the missing. Then you could check with him or his friends and neighbors to confirm he was the guy who shot himself.

The story of why the department feels their own should be treated differently becomes more important than the poor slob, who had the accident. But if editors let such actions go unchallenged they help public agencies build a wall to keep out citizen scrutiny.

Besides police reports, public record includes: deeds, minutes of public meetings, building permits, court pleadings, court dockets and anything that is kept as a public record on a regular basis. And if there is a mistake in the public record and you print it the courts won't hold you liable.

Thus an accurate news report based on court records that John Doe was convicted of murder, when in fact he was convicted of manslaughter, would not be actionable even though it would be defamatory and false. The reason: it was a fair and true report of the public record. In Chapter 4 of this book you will find a glossary of legal terms and what they mean. Make sure your editors and reporters know and understand them.

For example, if you say in a news report that John Doe was convicted of a felony for misappropriation of public funds when the document clearly states he was convicted of a misdemeanor for misappropriation of public funds you have just waded into the legal swamp with your throat exposed. You might get away with it because most readers don't know what the difference is between misdemeanors and felonies, but be aware of the exact language of the criminal charge and make sure you report it accurately.

Never, never, never rely on the oral assurance of the clerk. Remember the rule: get a copy of the document. If the clerk makes a mistake in telling you about a juicy case and you print it without getting the confirming document it becomes your mistake.

In the **Rouch** case, which is detailed in **Chapter 10** the news report in the Battle Creek Enquirer was based on conversations with officers of two different police agencies. When it came to trial neither agency recalled the conversations with the reporter leaving the reporter and the newspaper vulnerable on a critical point of the case.

The law is now very specific. It is the written document which creates the privilege not the oral notification of a public official.

One editor asked Dawn Phillips, who has handled newspaper law for the Michigan Press Association for the past 17 years, "You mean to tell me that if I run into the Chief of Police on the street and he tells me that John Smith, prominent citizen has just been arrested on selling cocaine, I can't use that information in the newspaper?" To which Dawn responded, "Of course you can. If you are willing to put the welfare of your newspaper in the hands of the police chief you may report his oral statements. BUT if the chief is mistaken or was just pulling your leg or he got the wrong John Smith, you will be responsible to the real John Smith for the consequences of your publication of a false charge." Remember, get the document.

There was one good result from **Rouch** **I** as we characterize it. (That is one good result other than paying for orthodontia and college educations for numerous children of attorneys.) Court proceedings are clearly public and official proceedings. This includes all hearings held in open court and probably administrative hearings as well.

The basis for this decision is rooted in English common law that held since court proceedings were open to the public and that anyone could come to see them, no harm was done by allowing publication of the contents of the proceeding. This tradition of openness plays an important part in every decision of the U.S. Supreme Court and the Michigan Supreme Court in determining public access. Thus the courts have concluded you have immunity from suit for reporting court proceedings so long as your report is fair and true.

Further court testimony is under oath and statements by attorneys are subject to Rules of Ethics for fairness and veracity. Thus the proceedings have an inherent quality of veracity.

One warning, what happens on the court house steps, no matter what they do on televison courtroom dramas, is not protected.

What happens if you are working for a daily and not a monthly and the court transcript won't be available by deadline? Be certain your notes are accurate and that they will substantially agree with the transcript when it becomes available. Don't simply rely on what some other reporter tells you happened. Other reporters hear things wrong. Check the statement or facts with both sides.

Just because you are doing a story on a trial doesn't necessarily mean you are safe. NBC found that out when they did a docudrama on a 1931 trial of the "Scottsboro Boys," nine black men, who were accused of raping two white women, one of whom was Street.

The famous trial and the surrounding characters were featured in the NBC presentation. But Ms. Street took exception to the portrayal of her character believing NBC implied she had perjured herself at the trial and that she was a prostitute. NBC was unable to shield itself claiming it had reported on an official proceeding because although the core facts were true it had taken great license with the characters. While the case was dismissed on other grounds relating to the public status of the plaintiff that will be discussed in Chapter 9 remember the report must be fair and true to take advantage of the privilege.

The Federal Sixth Circuit in holding against NBC on this issue stated that the privilege permitted for the publication of judicial proceedings is not satisfied where "the element of balance and neutrality is missing." **Victoria Price Street** **v** **National Broadcasting Co., 645 F.2d 1227 (6th Cir.1981).**

Criminal Complaint

The Court in Rouch I, (**Rouch v Enquirer & News of Battle Creek, 427 Mich 157; 398 NW2d 245 (1986)**) also seemed to assume that you could safely quote from the written document of a criminal complaint. So if you got a copy of the prosecutor's criminal complaint it would be considered part of the official proceeding or a public document. This protection would also appear to extend to an arrest warrant, a search warrant issued by the prosecutor and all documents subsequent to them in the criminal process.

Civil Complaint

Civil complaints are another story. You must make every effort to present both sides of such cases fairly. Under an old line of cases dating back to the late 1800's the Michigan Supreme Court said a report on a civil case was not protected until the case had reached a stage where it could be said the complaint was not frivolous.

In those days judges were more inclined to dismiss weak cases out of hand. Under current rules of "notice pleading" plaintiffs are only required to give basic notice of their claim they don't have to detail it so it is less likely a judge will have enough detail to dismiss a frivolous suit.

While civil pleadings including the complaint probably are covered by the term "documents of public record" as well as being part of the official proceeding you must be particularly careful in reporting allegations in a civil suit.

In a smaller community a complaint for medical malpractice, a complaint of theft of property, a complaint for misrepresentation can be devastating to the reputation of a defendant. If the complaint is merely the extension of a grudge unnecessary harm can be done. So until motions have been filed or a pretrial held, follow the advise of the Hill Street precinct desk sergeant. "Be careful out there folks."

If an attorney shows up in your office to hand deliver a copy of a complaint for a plaintiff be wary. Make sure the complaint has been filed and served. They are not simultaneous acts. The defendant or its proper agent must be served within 180 days of filing the complaint. It is well to have a copy of the pleading stamped with the filing notation of the court before reporting on the contents of a complaint. Remember, fairness is your guide.

Depositions

Depositions create a special problem. While they are taken under oath they no longer have to be filed with the Court. Even when they are filed they are often sealed to assure authenticity and can't be opened without a court order.

If a party to a suit files a portion of a deposition with the court as part of a motion or other pleading it can be used as news. If someone furnishes you a copy of a deposition outside the public record exercise caution. Make sure you receive the entire document not just selected excerpts; read the entire deposition before reporting anything contained in it and call the other side and ask for comment. Be pushy on this point. Explain what you have so the person or his attorney has a fair chance to respond. Don't settle with a single phone call and the catch-all caveat, "he was unavailable for comment."

Administrative Proceedings

Your privilege to report the contents of documents extends to administrative proceedings. Thus testimony taken at hearings of such administrative bodies as Workers' Compensation panels, Unemployment Compensation boards or the Michigan Employment Security Commission, a Tax Tribunal or Federal agencies and the like can be printed or reported. If the testimony is defamatory it still may be reported.

Local Governmental Meetings

The law also allows you to report on what public officials say at public meetings such as city council meetings, township board meetings, zoning commission meetings, boards of zoning appeals, school boards and the like.

On the other hand, be careful of statements from the audience by private citizens. These should be carefully reviewed. These folks are not under oath and they have no fiduciary duty like a public official to be truthful or measured in their speech. If, for example, a resident tells you in an aside at the zoning board meeting that his neighbor, who wants a zoning variance, is a crook, a cheat and a liar you better be careful about printing that charge without documentation to support it or giving the neighbor fair opportunity to respond, unless it was said on the record or included in the minutes of the public body.

The qualifying language in the statute on the proceedings of local government bodies says your privilege to report does not apply to a libel which you, your editor or publisher adds to the story or to anything else that is said or done at the time and place of the public and official proceedings.

For example, a Macomb Daily reporter thought he recognized the name of an individual charged with a series of crimes including fraud so he added some background about the individual and the company he owned to his story. It turned out it was the uncle of the man, who had been accused. Was the newspaper vulnerable to libel action? You bet your bippy.

Remarks made during the public comment section of any public meeting should qualify for protection because it is seen as part of the official proceeding by the Open Meetings Act. But again you should tread carefully because lawsuits have been filed over public comments by citizens at public meetings that were later reported in the newspaper.

For example, the Bay Voice, an excellent, free circulation, tabloid weekly in St. Clair County and The Macomb Daily were sued over remarks made by a School Superintendent about the leadership of a union with which the district was having a labor dispute. The newspapers eventually prevailed, but the Bay Voice, who was ably represented by Attorney Jane Briggs-Bunting, who also heads the Oakland University Journalism program, was unable to convince the Courts that the plaintiffs should be assessed legal fees for frivolous litigation.

Always fairness should be your watchword. Seeking a response from the object of remarks provides balance. Offering a opportunity to respond will often defuse the sting of emotional commentary.

There are also other defenses to the reporting of politically charged statements. One such defense discussed in Chapter 1 is hyperbole. Hyperbole is extravagant exaggeration. For example, if a citizen got up and said John Doe, a candidate for mayor, has the I.Q. of a fruit fly. No one would seriously believe that was a scientific observation. This concept will often prevent a successful suit for reporting political rhetoric. And the status of the individual criticized may make a difference. It is one thing to make jokes about Dan Quayle's spelling ability it might be another if you let someone similarly question the intellect of a person, who volunteers on a city centennial commission or a teacher.

Again, your libel attorney is happiest with absolute defenses and your privilege to report official proceedings is an absolute defense and should be the first response whenever feasible

Governmental Notices, Announcements, Written or Recorded Reports or Records Generally Available to the Public.

Press releases by a governmental agencies, government studies, statistical compilations and the conclusions drawn from them may be reported without liability for their defamatory content. The Legislature clarified this part of the statute in 1988 in direct response to Rouch I in which the courts concluded the statutory privilege of reporting did not extend to governmental notices.

However, there is one important warning you must heed. The document must be generally available to the public. If a Freedom of Information Act (FOIA) request would yield a denial of access to the document, your privilege to report its contents does not apply.

For example, if a City Council member "leaks" an opinion from the City Attorney about improper conduct by the City Manager and the possible criminal repercussions, you can't rely on the courts recognizing statutory privilege. An attorney's opinion involving personnel written to a public body is a document that would not have to be disclosed under a FOIA request hence no statutory protection.

You may still be able to publish the information under other statutory rulings, but your attorney can't hang his or her hat on the official proceedings act.

Police Log

A police log is a running compilation of the first impressions of officers on incidents that occur on a given day. It is a problem document. It should contain a warning label for reporters: "this log could be harmful to your legal costs."

Its purpose is to allow an officer coming on duty to know what has happened during the previous shift. Police will testify that the log is often inaccurate since it is not the official incident report, but simply a quick sketch of activities. Hence simple reports from the log can be dangerous.

The log may or may not meet the definition of a governmental written record generally available to the public. Some police departments don't let reporters see their logs. Some departments let some reporters view their logs, but will not let the general public see the log. If it is not available to the general public, which is true in most cases, the log is a less desirable source of confirming information. While it is an excellent source of leads and often contains valuable information, you should always confirm any facts you take from the log with other official documents or actions before publishing them.

Act or Action of a Public Body

You have the right to report accurately on an arrest before arraignment and the reporting of the police charge at the time of the arrest. The law says you are protected on reporting the actions of a public body as well as the written record of public actions. Stress the word accurate. Great care should be exercised to double check when reporting on arrests and charges which are not available in written form from authorities.

In fact, **Rouch I** has had such a chilling effect on the news media that most newsrooms in the state no longer report on criminal arrests before arraignments. And most libel defense attorneys endorse that approach unless the case falls under another protected category such as a public figure or public official. They suggest that you wait for a written document or the arraignment.

A good example of the changed climate can be cited at The Battle Creek Enquirer, the Gannett newspaper that suffered through a decade of agony over the Rouch cases.

In 1988 the Calhoun County Sheriff called the Enquirer newsroom to inform them that an arrest had been made in the tragic hit-and-run death of a popular 17-year-old Battle Creek student. The sheriff was proud of the break in the sad case. He noted the arrest was made possible through an anonymous tip the department received from the community Silent Observer program.

The Sheriff named the man being held. The Enquirer followed up the call and found out with a feeling of deja vu that the prosecutor had just learned of the arrest and had not seen any of the reports. Yet the sheriff had indicated a date on which the suspect would be arraigned.

The Enquirer news staff decided to withhold the name until he was arraigned. Shortly after the Sheriff called the newspaper received a press release detailing the same information: the name of the accused, the fact of the arrest and the police charge of "leaving the scene of a motor vehicle accident.

Under the new statute that press release is an official document and the newspaper could have used the name because of the privilege for reporting the contents of a "governmental announcement generally available to the public."

Both editors and reporters should follow this caveat: "When in Doubt, Leave it Out." It is not our business to destroy reputations, careers and peoples' personal lives. No news organization ever failed because it was so careful as to hold a story that extra hour, day, or week to confirm the damaging facts.

In the early 1980's the Vineland, N.J. Times Journal, then part of the news organization held by the owners of the Detroit News, went to extraordinary lengths to confirm a troublesome tip. The editors of the 28,000 circulation daily got a telephoned suggestion they check the police log of a township some 40 miles away, outside their circulation area. A reporter drove to the community and discovered the name of a Vineland zoning board member, who was active in Republican state politics, on the blotter. The charge was soliciting sex from a minor. He had been ticketed, but not detained in the incident. The reporter obtained a copy of the complaint.

Times Journal editors asked the official into their offices to present his side of the case. The accused appeared with his attorney and said it had all been a mistake. He said he was driving north to the state capital in Trenton during a rain storm and saw a poncho clad figure hitch hiking. He picked the person up. It wasn't until he was 20 or 30 miles up the road and his passenger had removed her poncho that he realized it was a girl. Since he was on his way to a meeting with the Governor he couldn't take time to return her to Vineland so he checked her into a nearby motel, telling her he would pick her up on his return trip and take her home. The girl after waiting at the motel for several hours called local police and they picked her up and returned her to Vineland.

When the public official returned to the motel an officer was waiting for him and ticketed him for soliciting. The man said, it was all a mistake and any kind of story would destroy him, his family and his political career. His attorney promised legal action if the newspaper published.

The editors sent the reporter back to the distant township to find the police officer. The officer, who issued the ticket was off duty so the reporter had to return again a day or two later. The reporter also visited the motel, which turned out to be one of those roadside places that featured mirrors in strange places and sex movies. The officer finally confirmed that not only did the public official check the teenager into the room he went to the room with her so he had to know it wasn't a locally owned Holiday Inn and when he came back rather than call her from the front desk he returned again to the room.

The newspaper did a story. It took three weeks from tip to publication. The man eventually pleaded guilty to lesser charges and no one got sued.

If you decide to print or air a story based on oral representations and you make a mistake such as the charge is second degree, not first degree; it is a misdemeanor not a felony; the arrested person was the son, not the father or grandfather; you could be in legal hot water.

On the other hand, as we've observed previously, if the mistake was contained in an accurate report of a written police incident report, you would be protected.

A Heading of the Report Which Is a Fair and True Headnote

We're talking about headlines here, folks. Probably the biggest single source of libel threats to news organizations. In essence the statute says the headlines are protected as long as they are fair and true. So don't make them sexy, make them accurate.

> **THIS PRIVILEGE SHALL NOT APPLY TO A LIBEL WHICH IS CONTAINED IN A MATTER ADDED BY A PERSON CONCERNED IN THE PUBLICATION OR CONTAINED IN THE REPORT OF ANYTHING SAID OR DONE AT THE TIME AND PLACE OF THE PUBLIC AND OFFICIAL PROCEEDING OR GOVERNMENTAL NOTICE**

That simply means the headline writer and the reporter better know the legal differences between forgery and uttering and publishing; between misdemeanors and felonies; between fraud and theft; between embezzling and misappropriation of funds. They need to know the difference between what is said within the proceeding and what is said on the courthouse steps or in the hallway. Only that which is said during the proceeding is covered by reporter's privilege.

If you get it wrong as a reporter or editor you have just rung the chums-Ching key again on your defense counsel's cash register. While we're not accustomed to thanking the Legislature for much of what it has done, we ought to express our appreciation daily for the absolute privilege they have accorded us under the statute. It is an invaluable tool for journalists reporting on governmental activity. Use it with care and have the courage to know when to report news that can't be documented, but is in the public interest. The last word has to be the editorial judgment of the reporter, the editor and the publisher of your news organization, not attorneys looking at the nuances of legal ramifications

A good newspaper attorney will tell you how to get something nailed down so he or she can defend you in court rather than simply tell you the dangers of publishing.

Chapter 6

Check List for Freedom of Information Request

1. **Try friendly persuasion first.**

2. **Keep notes on who you talk to and when if they are inclined to turn you down.**

3. **Go to the top if you have reasonable relations with the supervising public official and explain your dilemma: you need this information and you don't want to cost the agency money by having to involve attorneys. You now have a right of internal appeal.**

4. **Write your own letter. See Appendix I. Be specific about what you want.**

   A. **Consider whether the names of people involved are important to your search or whether statistics minus names would serve your purpose.**

   B. **Use relevant dates to keep the burden on the public body at a minimum.**

   C. **Remember that a public body can only charge you the incremental cost of complying with your request - paper and ink. However, you may want to volunteer to pay more for large document requests.**

5. **Don't look upon litigation as your ultimate weapon; it is too expensive. Involve an attorney only with supervisory approval.**

6. **Don't threaten litigation unless you have the support of your editor or publisher.**

7. **Be persistent. Government documents can protect you from a libel damages.**

Chapter 6

Freedom of Information

MCL 15.231, ET. SEQ.

One of the most powerful tools any reporter or editor can use in obtaining government information in Michigan is the Freedom of Information Act ("FOIA"). A second is the Open Meetings Act which will be dealt with in the next chapter. You will find copies of both acts and copies of a sample freedom of information request form in the Appendixes.

Sad to say reporters and editors use the FOIA tool (pronounced Foy-a by the folks who file lots of them) less frequently than Michigan's convicts did until recent legislation limited prisoner access.

Part of the problem is cost. While it doesn't cost anything to file a FOIA request or to look at the documents in question, getting a copy of the response and the non-response can. The statute specifically allows the public body to charge for the cost of the search and copying. when you actually receive copies to keep. It includes the actual cost of copying and the labor computed at the rate of the employee qualified to do the copying. That used to be the lowest paid clerk, but recent changes have opened the door to an agency charging a higher hourly rate for a computer expert.

It is important to make sure that any copies you feel you must have are useful. Fishing expeditions resulting in hundreds of documents can be expensive. Such requests also tend to irritate the public employee who responds to your request. Never say within earshot of the front desk clerk, "OH, this isn't what I wanted..

Two strong suggestions:

- Make conversation with the clerk and learn how information is kept to make your request as effective as possible.
- Ask to look at the responsive documents before you choose which ones require copying. You are only required to pay for copies you take with you.

The cost of obtaining data is rising, whether out of discovering the right to charge or whether out of a desire to discourage requests, public bodies are beginning to charge search and copying costs even for reporters. Ask to inspect documents before the copies are made. The Michigan Supreme Court has ruled that you have the right to see originals. Viewing originals allows you to make sure you really want the documents and gives you a reason to chat with a clerk and build a relationship as someone who doesn't waste the clerk's time. It also can save money.

It is often advisable to make an oral request to determine what exists before making your written request. If you get turned down you have to decide whether to pursue that request in the courts and many publishers are reticent to spend those dollars on legal fees. And if you file a written request and get turned down and don't follow up that convinces governmental agencies they can stonewall you.

You should use gentle persuasion with governmental clerks and secretaries before you run to your editor and request an attorney. It is good to know some of the key cases that support your request. And it is good to gently remind public employees that judges have been known to award legal fees to news organizations that have to resort to the courts to obtain information available under the act.

How the FOIA Works

There are two basic questions with regard to the use of FOIA.(1) Is the information I seek in the possession of government? (2) Are there any exemptions which government could use to prevent me from seeing the document?

Every piece of paper in the hands of government is a public document available for your use absent a specific exemption. Government is the repository of a tremendous amount of information. Almost any story you do can benefit from government files whether because your subject matter is licensed or is the subject of a government inquiry or has interacted with government creating a government record. Police reports, traffic reports, Formal complaints against doctors and lawyers are open to the public; court files are open to the public; the amount of newsprint in garbage dumps is a government statistic; mug shots, environmental reports, pounds of potatoes grown in Michigan, - all of these are data available from the government.

By data in the hands of government, FOIA means in any form. Writing includes computer files, electronic bytes, tapes and of course good old fashioned paper.

The next question to look at is the list of exemptions in Section 13 of the Act. Sometimes careful wording of a FOIA request can avoid the application of an exemption that will prevent you from getting data. For example, charges of police misconduct are always very serious and police departments are understandably, even if illegally, reluctant to share the details of the charges and the investigation thereof. One approach is to ask for all documents relating to charges against officer John Doe for an incident occurring on Christmas day. This often will get you a heavily redacted copy of some documents and darn little of anything else. However, if instead you ask for copies of all complaints against police officers for the last five years and indicate that you are not interested in the identity of the officers, you will often eliminate the application of exemptions for invasion of privacy. Usually you will be able to tell which details go to the most recent event and you will have a history of charges of police misconduct and the official response thereto, which may in the end be a better story.

There are exemptions from a to y. They include matters the release of which would constitute a clearly unwarranted invasion of privacy to answers to qualifying exams for licensure to identification of informants, See Appendix 12, Sec. 13 of FOIA for a list of the exemptions. But government has a lot of interesting information in its possession and all you need is FOIA and an imaginative mind to find information to bolster your story, regardless of the topic.

How to Make a FOIA Request.

Under recent amendments to the FOIA requests must be made in writing in order gain the procedures of the Act. A sample FOIA request is contained at the back of this book at Appendix 1. Nothing magic here folks, just the obvious.

Some newspapers provide their reporters with fill in the blanks copies of a FOIA request so a staffer, who has a verbal request rebuffed can start the process immediately.

The most important thing besides putting it in writing is that you should keep a copy of any letter for your files and in case legal action becomes necessary.

You also have to determine to whom you should make your request. The law requires public bodies to designate an information officer. It can be anybody. Advice: make friends with the information officer! If they are not friendly then you must develop a strategy for working with them. Discuss it with your supervisor.

I Made My Request; Now What Do I Do?

Public bodies have five business days to respond to your request. As Ben has suggested above check with the lucky recipient of your request and find out whether or not your request is likely to get the information you are seeking and whether or not the request is unduly burdensome. Also keep a copy of your request and tickle your calendar when the response is due.

I Got a Response; Now What Do I Do?

If your response appears complete, say thank you! But if the response has blacked out information or if the response says that you can not have the entire document, you need to take a second look at your response.

One of the most important sections of the FOIA is Section 14 which says that a public body must separate exempt material from non-exempt material. This means that if an entire document is denied, you should ask the public body whether or not each and every word of the document is exempt from disclosure. For example, if you made a request for the resume of a public employee, the FOIA allows the public body to withhold the social security number of the employee. If the social security number appears in the resume, the public body cannot withhold the entire document because one fact in the document can be withheld legally.

Next you should take a look at the case of **The Evening News** v **The City of Troy, 417 Mich 481; 339 NW2d 421 (1983)**. Every editor and reporter in Michigan should be familiar with a 1983 case between The Detroit News and the city of Troy and the eventual Michigan Supreme Court decision which ruled that police incident reports and the names of officers involved in them are public record unless there is a particular reason why release of such information would hamper an ongoing investigation. Additionally the court strongly supported the statute's requirement that a public body has a duty to separate information that is public record from such information that needs to be withheld to guarantee the integrity of an investigation.

The case between The Detroit Evening News and the City of Troy is an example of the kind of double talk we spoke of above with regard to seeking sensitive information from government.

The Supreme Court set down the following standard for analyzing a claim of exemption from FOIA disclosure:

1. The burden of proof is on the party claiming exemption from disclosure, i.e. the public body.

2. Exemptions must be interpreted narrowly.

3. The public body shall separate the exempt and nonexempt material and make the nonexempt material available for examination and copying. **MCL § 15.244(1); MSA § 4.1801(14)(1);**

4. Detailed affidavits describing the matters withheld must be supplied by the agency.

5. Justification of exemption must be more than "conclusory," i.e. simple repetition of statutory language. A bill of particulars is in order. Justification must indicate factually how a particular document, or category of documents, interferes with law enforcement proceedings.

6. The mere showing of a direct relationship between records sought and an investigation is inadequate.

417 Mich at 502 see also **Nicita** v **Detroit, 194 Mich App 657; 487 NW2d 814 (1992).**

Generic denials thus do not satisfy the FOIA. The high court concluded a public body must indicate factually and in detail how a particular document or category of documents satisfies the exemption; mere conclusory allegations are not sufficient.

Editors and reporters should also be aware that the city of Troy was ordered to reimburse the Detroit News for $40,000 in legal costs that it spent in pursuing the case for more than four years through Michigan's courts. We have attached a form outlining the case to be used with appropriate modification for the recalcitrant public official. (See Appendix 1).

The News didn't pursue the case to make the city of Troy suffer. It pursued it because it believed police officials have no right to treat their own officers differently than they would average citizens.

The facts of the case are these:

David Prior, a Troy resident, had been having trouble with theft or vandalism on his van which he kept parked in his driveway. He had reported this to police and he called the police department to tell them he was going to stake out his van the night of July 30 to see if he could catch the culprits. So he hid himself in his parked van with a pellet gun. Early on July 31 two officers responding to a radio report that there might be a theft occurring in the van saw Prior with the pellet rifle. One of the officers shot and killed him.

Both officers and several other investigating officers filed incident reports describing the events leading to the killing. But the police department and city officials refused to release the names of the officers or the reports citing an ongoing investigation as the reason. Each week for three weeks a News reporter requested the information and finally confirmed the newspaper's requests in writing on Aug. 22. It was refused by the Troy police chief, the City and the Oakland County prosecutor's office. The newspaper's editors reasoned that if average citizen John Smith had accidentally shot and killed his neighbor similarly staked out in a van that the police would release John Smith's name. Therefore they had no basis for withholding the names of the two officers and their reports.

It took more than four years to prove that point, but the case sets a precedent for reporters dealing with police and governmental officials in every city and hamlet in Michigan. Each reporter on your staff should be familiar with the basic details of the Troy case and gently remind police and public officials of them if they seem reluctant to provide information that should be released. That doesn't mean that you are going to get everything you want when you want it, but it can be a useful pry bar. If you need to make a formal complaint we suggest the letter attached with appropriate modifications.

What Should I Be Able to Get And What Will Be a Problem?

Personal Information

The most common exemption claimed by public bodies is that the release of the information would constitute a clearly unwarranted invasion of individual privacy. Generally, the privacy right protected by this exemption is the same as the common law privacy right for public disclosure of embarrassing private facts discussed in Chapter 2. Therefore, if the information you are seeking could be the basis for a successful invasion of privacy lawsuit, it would likely be exempt from disclosure under FOIA. However, the FOIA exemption is even more narrow as it is limited only to "clearly unwarranted" invasions of private information, such as a low level public employee's medical history. Yet, the Michigan Supreme Court has recently indicated that there is a distinction between information in possession of government agencies concerning private citizens and information concerning government employees. Information concerning private citizens is more likely to qualify for the exemption. **Mager** v **Dep't of State Police, 460 Mich 134; 595 NW2d 142 (1999)**.

Police Reports

As we all learned from the Rouch case, getting a copy of a police report can be a crucial defense if we are sued for libel. Therefore, maintaining access under the FOIA should be a primary concern for all reporters. A denial of a FOIA request is a serious matter.

Police reports are subject to a number of exemptions: under investigation, interfering with fair trial rights, invasion of privacy, revealing informants and the like. Although it is wise to be understanding of law enforcement needs, do not be lulled into accepting their assurances that you are not entitled to a report. Under Evening News you are entitled to a particularized list of the types of documents and information being withheld. This allows you to determine whether or not you agree with the assessment of the public body that you are not entitled to the information requested.

Deprive a Person of a Right to a Fair Trial

Constitute an Unwarranted Invasion of Personal Privacy

This exemption differs from the privacy exemption discussed above only in the omission of the word "clearly". Release of the information must still constitute the release of personal information and must be unwarranted, in order to justify withholding the information. Although it is a slightly less stringent test, it is still difficult for information to meet the requirements of this exemption. The information must be of embarrassing, intimate private facts.

In **People v DeLisle, 202 Mich App 658, 509 NW2d 885, (Mich 1993)**, the Michigan Court of Appeals set forth the parameters of the fair trial right as juxtaposed with pretrial publicity. The Court of Appeals quoted the U.S. Supreme Court for the general proposition that "juror exposure to information about a state defendant's prior convictions or to news account of the crime with which he is charged" cannot alone presumptively deprive the defendant of due process. The Court of Appeals discussed the case of **Estes v Texas, 381 U.S. 532, 85 S. Ct. 1628, 14 L. Ed. 2d 543 (1965)** where the pretrial hearings were carried live on radio and television. There were at least twelve cameramen in the courtroom during the proceedings and cables and wires were snaked everywhere, and the activities of television crews and news photographers created considerable disruption. In that setting, the Supreme Court found prejudice and reversed the conviction.

Likewise in **Sheppard v Maxwell, 384 333, 86 S. Ct. 1507, 16 L.Ed.2d 600 (1966)**, the defendant's conviction was reversed where the coroner with the prosecutor and two bailiffs held a televised three day inquest of the defendant in a school gymnasium during which the defendant was publicly searched and the defendant's attorney was not allowed to participate. These are the kinds of egregious circumstances in which a defendant's right to a fair trial is violated.

Even the existence of preconceived notions regarding guilt or innocence is not enough to rebut the presumption of impartiality where the juror says that he can put those opinions aside. In the **DeLisle** case, there were 37 articles published in August of 1989 shortly after DeLisle drove off the Ambassador bridge killing his four children. There were 15 articles in September, eight in October and six in November and four articles published in February, one in March, none in April and two in May before the trial and 28 published during the trial in June.

Significantly in **DeLisle**, the defendant had confessed to killing his children and the confession was printed in the newspapers six months before the trial. The confession was ruled inadmissible because of the coercive situation into which the defendant had been placed. Nonetheless, despite the fact that an inadmissible confession had been disclosed and printed in the newspaper, the jurors indicated that they were not biased against the defendant. The Court found that there had been a fair trial notwithstanding the pretrial publicity.

Identify a Confidential Source
Settlements of Lawsuits Involving The Government

Secret settlements by governmental agencies are illegal. The Michigan Press Association Hotline gets used frequently with this question: Can a public body legally deny access to an agreement settling a lawsuit against the public body?

The answer is that there is no exemption under FOIA which would allow withholding of a settlement agreement. There is no provision for agreements for confidentiality. Happily, the recent case of **Christine Bradley v Saranac School District**, held among other things that nothing in the FOIA gives public bodies the right to agree to seal documents. The court held that unless there is a specific statute indicating that the document may be sealed, the document must be open subject to the exemptions under Section 13. Generally there is no provision that would allow a settlement to be sealed.

One way to get around any objection in a hurry is to simply ask to look at all checks written to a party or the attorneys for the party. There are no exemptions for financial records. And that is a mandate of the state Constitution.

Article 9 Section 23 of the Michigan Constitution provides: All financial records, accountings, audit reports and other reports of public moneys shall be public records and open to inspection.

David Ashenfelter, a reporter for The Detroit Free Press, sued the City of Detroit for information on secret settlements in Oakland County (in which he resides) and won. He had made numerous requests for information on the settlement of lawsuits by Detroit.

It is not uncommon practice for litigants to agree to seal settlement terms of a lawsuit, especially the amount of money paid. Defendants argue that the only way to assure that the settlement is not seen as an admission of liability is to keep it secret.

Defendants also argue that sealing the amount of the settlement discourages additional lawsuits. However, given the number of lawsuits filed in this country and the increasing size of verdicts, it seems unlikely that any empirical evidence of this conclusion can be found.

Whatever the justification or fear of the parties there are additional concerns when a public body is involved. When a public body settles a lawsuit, public funds are used. The public has a right to know about how its officials are handling the moneys they have entrusted to them.

Public bodies may respond that it is not their money, but that of an insurance company. But we all know what happens when your insurance company has to pay a sizable claim on your behalf. Rates go up. Additionally the insurance company is merely the agent of the public body. FOIA applies to agreements or contracts which a municipality executes so you should not let your local officials sidestep the issue. Settlement agreements should be approved at an open public meeting.

This issue should be a high priority for newspaper coverage. Litigation involving your local governmental agencies should be reported thoroughly and you should pursue your right to get information which the public needs to make decisions on the effectiveness of their leaders.

In addition you and your editors should be alert to Michigan Press Association advisories on legislative attempts to dilute or weaken the Open Meetings Act and the Freedom of Information Act. Attempts to weaken the acts occur as frequently as robins return to Michigan in the spring. If your local lawmakers are involved you can play a key role in getting them to re-think their positions if you editorialize when you disagree with them.

Prominent Michigan libel attorney Herschel P. Fink, a partner in the Detroit firm of Honigman, Miller, Schwartz and Cohn, and a former night city editor at the Detroit News points out that the principle of free public access to information long pre-dates the 1977 Michigan FOIA Act. He and co-author Darlene Darnell cite three cases in their 1989 publication "TAPPING Officials' Secrets in MICHIGAN": **Nowack v Auditor Gen., 243 Mich 200; 219 NW 749 1928; Burton v Tuite, 78 Mich 363; 44 NW 282 (1889) and Booth Newspapers v Muskegon Probate Judge,15 Mich App 203; 166 NW2d 546 (1968)** as key examples of decisions in favor of information being available to the public.

The **Nowack** decision enforced a newspaper's right of inspection by court order and cited the **Burton v Tuite** decision as an example of the state's commitment to the principle of free access, according to Fink and Darnell. And this was echoed again in 1968 in the Booth Newspapers case against a Muskegon probate judge in which the court said: "The fundamental rule in Michigan. . . is that citizens have the general right of free access to, and public inspection of, public records. . . .The Nowack decision has "placed Michigan at the vanguard of those states holding that a citizen's accessibility to public records must be given the broadest possible effect," the two writers concluded.

Michigan penal statutes provide for penalties for officials who don't reasonably offer the opportunity to examine and copy public records, according to Fink and Darnell. They cite **Mich. Comp. Laws Ann. Sec. 750.491** (West 1968):

> Provided, that the custodian of said records and files may make such reasonable rules and regulations with reference to the inspection and examination of them as shall be necessary for the protection of said records and files, and to prevent interference with the regular discharge of the duties of such officer. .."

You also should plan to take a pencil with you or a notebook computer as the statute, passed in a day when fountain ink pens were in vogue also, provides public officials can't let you use them to copy materials for fear you'll spill ink on them. That only says that messy reporters are not a new phenomenon.

Notwithstanding all of the foregoing, and the fact that the Supreme Court laid down some specific directives for public bodies for FOIA requests in The Evening News case, it is a good idea to know the law and use non-confrontational ways of obtaining information that you can write your story with the use of public documents and meet your deadline. Litigation is not swift justice. The Evening News case took from 1979 To 1983. Most deadlines in newspaper newsrooms are a little tighter than three years!

Do Federal Agencies Have to Respond to a FOIA Request?

Yes, Virginia there is a Federal FOIA! But it is a different version of the right to know. For example, under the Federal FOIA, information need only be an invasion of privacy, not a "clearly unwarranted" invasion of privacy in order to be exempt. Also there is a Federal Privacy

Act which creates numerous exemptions of information about individuals that would not be applicable in Michigan to Michigan documents.

On the other hand, federal officials just as state officials must furnish photos of suspects arrested and charged in federal cases. This was established in 1996 when the U.S. government finally gave up attempting to claim that such photos were private. The Detroit Free Press had requested photos of eight persons arrested in a federal gambling investigation of the Wolverine Golf Club in Mt. Clemens in 1993, who had appeared in open court. The U.S. attorneys argued they should not have to release them as they were an invasion of privacy. Eventually U.S. District Judge Anna Diggs Taylor ruled against the government in 1994 and awarded the newspaper almost $30,000 in attorney fees. The government appealed and was turned down by a 2-1 federal appellate panel at the 6th Circuit Court of Appeals in Cincinnati. They sought a hearing before the full court and got turned down and in June 1996 they decided to abandon the position and turned over the photos. By that date all of the persons accused in the case had been found not guilty, but as Fink pointed out in the Free Press, "I think this is an important Freedom of Information case in that it does define the concept of privacy."

The Free Press is to be congratulated on insuring access to the mug shots of arrestees in state and federal detention.[1]

This treatise does not cover the Federal FOIA

For a list of web sites, phone numbers and other resources that can aid you in your pursuit and understanding of the state and federal FOIA laws see Appendix 6.

1. "Free Press granted access to federal suspects" photos, Detroit Free Press, June 15, 1996, page 13A.

Chapter 7

Open Meetings Act (OMA) Check List

1. A public body is a body given power to exercise governmental or proprietary authority or perform a governmental or proprietary function.

2. All decisions by a public body must be at a meeting open to the public.

3. All deliberations of a public body toward a decision must be open unless specifically exempted under section 8 of the OMA or another statute.

4. All meetings open to the public must be noticed in accordance with the OMA.

5. A meeting of a public body consists of the gathering of a quorum of the members of the public body although chance meetings or social gatherings not designed to avoid the act are not meetings subject to the OMA.

6. All meetings of a public body shall be held in a place available to the general public.

7. The right of a person to attend a meeting of a public body includes the right to tape-record, to videotape, to broadcast live on radio, and to telecast live on television the proceedings of a public body at a public meeting.

8. A person shall not be required as a condition of attendance at a meeting of a public body. to register or otherwise provide his or her name or other information or otherwise to fulfill a condition precedent to attendance.

9. A person shall be permitted to address a meeting of a public body under rules established and recorded by the public body.

10. A committee of a public body may be required to comply with the OMA, if it is delegated a government or proprietary function, such as making recommendations on five finalists for police chief, the

committee is a public body in its own rights and must hold its meetings open to the public.

11. **Most meetings of public bodies should be open, Although some may be closed.**

12. **Some public bodies are exempt from the OMA by statute including for example the state teacher tenure commission, the worker's compensation board, the public service commission and others.**

13. **Minutes must be kept of both open and closed meetings. Proposed minutes shall be available not more than 8 business days after the meeting. Approved minutes shall be available not later than 5 business days after the meeting at which the minutes are approved.**

14. **Minutes of closed sessions are not available unless you file a civil suit to get them disclosed. The closed meeting minutes can be destroyed a year and a day after the approval of minutes of the regular meeting at which the closed session was approved.**

15. **Meetings to discuss purchase or lease of land, for strategy and negotiation sessions in regard to a collective bargaining agreement and to discuss material exempt by law such as written legal opinions can be closed.**

16. **Meetings can be closed for an agency to consult with its attorney on pending litigation if it would have a detrimental effect on the settlement position of the public body**

17. **Meetings to review applications for appointment to a public office or public employment may be closed if the candidate requests it. However, all interviews by a public body for employment or appointment to a public office must be open.**

18. **Partisan caucuses of members of the state legislature may be closed.**

19. **Meetings of public bodies must also be held pursuant to notice as set forth in section 4 of the act. Even closed meetings must be noticed.**

20. **Upon written request, a public body, at the same time a public notice of a meeting is posted shall provide a copy of the public notice of that**

meeting to any newspaper published in the state and to any radio and television station located in the state, free of charge.

21. **If a public body moves to close what you believe should be a public meeting you should advise them in a friendly manner of your belief and ask they get an opinion from their attorney.**

22. **Check copies of "Michigan's Freedom of Information and Open Meetings Act," which should be available in your newsroom. The Attorney General has issued more than 50 opinions on various aspects of the Open Meetings Act.**

23. **You may file a lawsuit to enjoin closed sessions in violation of the act and you can collect your attorney fees if you win.**

Chapter 7

Open Meetings

The intent of the Michigan Open Meetings Act passed in 1977 and modeled after similar acts in a number of other states is to have government operate in the open so the public can know what is going on. It is keynoted by Section 3 of the law which states in part:

"All meetings of a public body shall be open to the public and shall be held in a place available to the general public. All persons shall be permitted to attend any meeting except as otherwise provided in this act. The right of a person to attend a meeting of a public body includes the right to tape-record, to videotape, to broadcast live on radio, and to telecast live on television the proceedings of a public body at a public meeting." MCL 15.263

The coverage of the law is broad, including the Michigan Legislature as well as legislative or governing bodies of all cities, villages, townships, charter townships, county units of government, local and intermediate school districts, governing boards of community colleges, state colleges and universities; special boards and commissions created by law such as public hospital authorities, road commissions, health boards and zoning boards.

Some key questions: is the body created by law; does its authority come from a statute, a city charter or a resolution of another public body. If yes, it's a public body. Who appoints its members? If they are elected at a public election, it is a public body. If they are appointed by a public body it is probably a public body.

Exempt bodies

The courts in their administrative discussions or while exercising rule making authority and police agencies in administrative discussions are not subject to the Open Meetings Act. Some other bodies are exempt under certain circumstances and some meetings can be properly closed to the public. For example when they are deliberating the merits of a case these agencies are exempt: Workers Compensation Appeal Board, the Employment Security Appeals Board, the Michigan Veterans Trust Fund Board, the Teacher Tenure Commission when acting as a board of review and Employment Relations Commission arbitration panels.

Universities

Meetings of State University Boards of Trustees are generally subject to the Open Meetings Act. However, in June 1999, the Michigan Supreme Court ruled that the application of the Open Meetings Act to university presidential searches was unconstitutional under The Michigan Constitution. **Federated Publications, Inc. v Board of Trustees of Michigan State University, 460 Mich 75; 594 NW2d 491 (1999).** This decision seems to be limited to meetings related to a university presidential search. Unfortunately, there is language in the decision that could be interpreted to exempt university boards from the Open Meetings Act for all purposes except where they meet in self-defined "formal sessions". It remains for the universities and ultimately the courts to determine how far this ruling will extend.

Public Business

The purpose of the Open Meetings Act requirement is to let the elector know what the government is up to. Michigan therefore requires that all decisions of public bodies be made at an open meeting. Nor will Michigan law allow a public body to meet in open session, but vote by secret ballot or discuss matters through the use of pseudonyms. Thus, in one case a school board was found to have violated the law when they discussed misconduct of certain students and identified the students only by their student numbers and not their names. The courts have been strict in requiring compliance with not only the strict language of the Open Meetings Act, but the spirit of the Act.

The Act also requires that all deliberations toward a decision be held in a meeting open to the public unless the situation falls within one of the eight factual situations described in Section 8 of the Act. But all actual decisions of public bodies in Michigan must be made at an open meeting. Closed sessions may be held for deliberations, but never for decision making.

Closed Meetings

Meetings can be closed to: consider the dismissal, suspension or disciplining of a public officer or official if the named person requests a closed hearing; or similarly in dealing with a student if the student's parent or guardian requests a closed hearing; for strategy and negotiation sessions connected to negotiating a collective bargaining agreement; to consider the purchase or lease of property up until the time an option or the property is obtained; to consult with its attorney on pending litigation if an open meeting would have a detrimental financial effect on the public body; to review employment applications or applications for public employment if the candidate requests confidentiality; to hold partisan caucuses of members of the state legislature; to consider material exempt from disclosure by state or federal statute.

In order to close a meeting two-thirds of the members of a public body must vote yes in a roll call and the purpose for closing the meeting must be stated.

All that said you should be aware that the Open Meetings Act is violated almost daily somewhere in Michigan and there are numerous public agencies looking for ways to avoid the Act which is detailed in **Appendix 10**. In addition, there are many State Attorney General and Court Opinions that bear on the Act. They can be found in free brochures distributed by the office of the Attorney General, most legislators and the Michigan Freedom of Information Committee.

What Public Agencies Can't Do

Here are some things which public agencies can't do:

Interview candidates for an appointment or job in closed session if a quorum (in most cases a majority) of the members of an agency are present . The Michigan Legislature modified this for university president searches in late 1996. Only the finalists must be interviewed in public. And there is a move in the Legislature in 1997 to extend the mantle of secrecy to other public office holders.

Vote by secret ballot at a public meeting.

Listen to presentations by department heads and administrators of the public body in closed session when a quorum is present.

Hold meetings a distance from the governmental unit that would make it difficult or inconvenient for citizens served to attend.

Withhold the minutes of a meeting of a Board of Education which must list the name of a student expelled for repeated rules and regulations violations.

Call themselves committees to avoid the requirements of the Act.

However, if a quorum of a public agency should meet accidentally at a social gathering or conference they are not in violation of the law as long as they don't discuss and take action on public business.

Meeting Notice Requirements

Under the Act regular meetings of a public body should be posted for the year within 10 days of the first meeting for the year and if there is a change in the regular meetings it should be posted within three days of the meeting at which the change was approved. Special meetings require 18 hours notice in most cases.

Minutes

Minutes must be kept of open meetings and also of closed meetings and retained by the clerk of the public body. Closed meeting notes will remain secret except in the case a civil action forces them to be disclosed. Closed meeting notes can be destroyed a year and a day after the approval of the minutes of the regular meeting at which the closed session was approved. Proposed minutes must be available for public inspection within 8 business days after a public meeting and approved minutes must be available within 5 business days after a meeting a which they were approved.

Electronic Meetings

A number of devices have been employed by various agencies to attempt to meet without violating the law. For example, University of Michigan regents thought they could discuss business by E-Mail. However, the Attorney General has ruled that such E-Mail is subject to Freedom of Information requests and is public record.

Committees

In a recent decision of the court of appeals, the courts finally stated what we knew and public bodies refused to acknowledge: committees of public bodies that are delegated significant governmental function are public bodies and must hold open meetings and otherwise comply with the act. The act clearly covers committees and subcommittees. But the attorney general confused the issue by writing an opinion that said that advisory bodies did not have to hold open meetings. The courts disagreed with this analysis and adopted the plain language of the Open Meetings Act that committees who are given significant authority are required to open their meetings. As of the winter of 1997 the case has been appealed but remains the law.

Enforcing the Act

Every citizen has the right to sue a public body to force them to open meetings and you can collect attorney fees if you get an injunction against similar conduct in the future. But be careful. If the public body says "so sorry! We won't do that again!" there will be no attorney fees. Courts do not always order governmental defendants to pay attorney costs and that is something to think about when you are spending the news room budget.

Penalties for Violating the Act

If a public official intentionally breaks the law he or she can face a fine of up to $1,000 and a second offense within the same term of office could result in a fine of up to $2,000 or one year in jail or both. The public official is also personally liable for actual and exemplary damages up to $500 plus court costs and attorney fees.

Invalidating Decisions

It is also possible to sue to invalidate a decision of a public body if it was made in violation of the act. Usually newspapers do not get involved in the decision making process. But it is one of the possible remedies. However, 30-day and 60-day limitations on the filing of such lawsuits makes them difficult and the public body can simply avoid such a lawsuit by holding an open meeting and voting on the disputed issue again.

Chapter 8

Handling Complaints Check List

1. How you handle the first contact from an unhappy reader is crucial. It will probably be by phone. Listen carefully. Be friendly, courteous and kind.

2. Do not be defensive or thin-skinned. Remember the proverb, a soft answer turneth away wrath. A good response to practice is, "I'm sorry you feel that way. Please explain exactly what you object to in the story." *Acknowledge their feelings not their facts*.

3. Identify the facts in question and offer to check any that are in dispute. Offer to call the person back with a response and then do so after briefing your supervisor and getting his or her ok.

4. Make sure your news organization has a clearly stated corrections and clarifications policy and put the corrections or clarifications in a place where readers can find them easily.

5. If you get an official demand for a retraction from an attorney make sure your supervisor and attorney take over any negotiations for a retraction. Under Michigan law plaintiffs have a year in which to demand a retraction; after that a libel suit is time barred.

6. Most suits are filed to restore reputation not get money. Make sure you have not unfairly cast doubt on someone's reputation. If there are three John Smiths in your small city it can't hurt to run a clarification that the person charged with embezzlement is not related to John X. Smith the banker or John Q. Smith the financial consultant.

7. Nine out of 10 persons who sued in an Iowa study were men.

8. About six out of 10 libel actions are lost by the news outlet at the trial court level when a jury of the plaintiff's peers get to express their opinion of the news media. About 60 percent of those are reversed on appeal. But it isn't cheap to let it go that far.

Chapter 8

How to Handle Libel Complaints

Who can sue you for libel? Anyone can and anyone will.

A couple of respected Michigan attorneys, who have handled newspaper law and libel cases for years made this observation about libel plaintiffs: "Assuming they have not been ignored at the time of their initial complaint, libel plaintiffs tend to be paranoid, egotistical, self-centered and thin skinned."

The problem is that also describes a lot of newspaper editors and reporters in terms of their reaction to complaints. We are going to give you some simple tips on how to respond to complaints and profile the typical libel plaintiff so when you are gathering facts for your story you can be even more careful in those areas where the subject fits the likely libel suit. It is sort of like the airlines identifying folks they think might be hijackers.

We have relied heavily for our profile on our own anecdotal experience and on material gathered by the University of Iowa as part of the Iowa Libel Research Project and published in 1987 in the book "Libel Law and the Press, Myth and Reality," by Randall P. Bezanson, Gilbert Cranberg and John Soloski. It was part of an effort to establish alternative dispute resolution to libel suits.

"There was no thought or hint of laughter on the cold gray dawn of the morning after," according to a bit of poetry Ben's dad used to quote. And many complaints about accuracy, libel and defamation occur on the cold, gray dawn of Monday mornings because you chose to print your expose on Sunday of the National Widget Factory and how they have been providing local officials various bribes to overlook the pollution of the Onceatonic River.

Your assignment whether you choose to accept it or not is to greet the caller cheerfully with courtesy and concern for the problem as they see it.

A significant number of legal complaints can be short stopped by letting the person vent. That doesn't mean you have to agree with them, but don't hesitate to agree to look into the complaint and get back to them.

Don't be defensive and don't get into an argument with the caller. Of course, since we have already suggested that many of you are too defensive about having your Pulitzer candidate baby questioned as just another ugly effort to sell newspapers that may be about as useful as telling a person, "just because you're paranoid doesn't mean that people aren't out to get you."

Editors should consider assigning someone to be the first line of cooperation on complaint calls. You note we did not say, the first line of defense. Pick a mature veteran, who likes people and has concern for basic fairness, whether it is a secretary, a receptionist, a reporter or an editor. It may be someone who is not in the newsroom chain of command.

At the Detroit News in the late 1980's Executive Sports Editor Herb Boldt, a former President of the Michigan Press Association took on the responsibility as a Reader Representative along with his other special project duties. He had answering machines to take calls when he wasn't there and one of our best secretaries Terry Dobson worked with him. Herb had spent years covering the police beat, directing reporters on the metro desk and running the sports operation and he basically likes people.

We'll never know how many libel actions were dropped before they even got started, but we do know that the readers appreciated knowing there was a good professional they could turn to if they thought they had been abused.

Listen sympathetically to what the caller has to say. Take good notes and get telephone numbers. Promise to look into the matter and re-contact the complainant. Then follow through. Start by talking to the reporter and the editor who handled the story. Get all the facts. Then recommend a course of action to the publisher or another supervisor.

One problem is that alleged libels are seldom clear cut and drafting something satisfactory to the complainant difficult. The complainant wishes to be vindicated; the newspaper wishes to be accurate. The two goals are often in conflict. You should focus on what the reader needs to know to understand the story fairly. If you believe it is a seriously damaging libel any clarification or correction must be written with an eye to what a jury would think. If there is a strong likelihood it will go to court will the jury view it as an admission of fault or falsity? Will it re-enforce the libel? Great care must be taken in drafting a follow-up on a story and if it appears to you and the publisher that there is a strong possibility of a suit, then the follow-up story should be discussed with your attorney. Sometimes a clarification or retraction is simply not possible.

But don't be afraid to run corrections or clarifications. Our job is to inform the public and to be fair. You will only enhance the reputation of the newspaper if you have the courage to be honest and fair.

Have a corrections and clarifications policy and don't be afraid to print enough background with a correction so the reader can understand the context.

At the Detroit News, Ben once ordered a correction onto Page One with a multi-columned headline over a flawed business story on Burroughs that caused stock prices to drop. The company shelved plans to seek legal remedies and thanked the newspaper for its action.

They blew up copies of the correction and posted them on entrance doors to the company headquarters with the headline: "We Asked for it and We Got It."

Hardly anyone outside of Burroughs remembers the error, but a lot of media professionals remember the News had class enough to admit its mistake promptly and forthrightly.

Now let's look at who is likely to sue you. It is likely to be a man, who is over 35, who has lived in the community more than 10 years, who is or has been in public life as a candidate or an elected official or works for a government agency, or else he is a businessman or white collar worker, who earns more than $25,000 a year. He is going to be outraged and angry and concerned about restoring his reputation.

Almost nine out of ten plaintiffs in the Iowa study were men. Three out of four of them had lived in the community more than 10 years and one out of three were lifelong community residents. About four out of ten made more than $50,000 a year in 1987 dollars. More than half were college grads and three out of four of them were married.

Four out of ten described themselves as "highly visible" and three out of ten were public employees. Two of ten had held elective office or had been candidates. About one in four were professionals and about one in four were business owners, managers or white collar workers.

Most suits are filed to restore reputation. In about 60 percent of the cases studied by the Iowa project the plaintiff contacted the media before filing an action. All but one of those contacted said that anger was a factor in their decision to sue. In about six out of ten of these the plaintiff was angered by the response and most of the rest were dissatisfied. The authors concluded that in many cases the decision to sue was based on the way the plaintiff was treated rather than on the substantive reaction to the complaint.

". . . Two overriding elements appear generally applicable across the spectrum of cases and plaintiffs," the Iowa Project authors write. "Virtually all of the plaintiffs were chiefly disturbed about the alleged falsity of the published report, and its consequent impact on their reputation. Their reason for suit might have been expressed in terms of reputation, money, or vengeance at the time they decided to sue, but underlying that decision in virtually every instance was a perception that falsity was at the bottom of their grievance, and their action was directed at correcting that falsity."

The Iowa professors also found that the act of filing the suit satisfied to some extent the needs of the complainants and represented a sort of public vindication. Under Michigan law plaintiffs have one year in which to proceed with a libel action after an offensive story has run.

The facts show that as many as six out of ten libel actions are lost at the trial court level in Michigan and at least 60 percent of those are reversed in favor of the newspapers on appeal. But that is an expensive process and in our pursuit of the truth and service to the public we might pay better attention to those folks, who call in and say, "You got that wrong."

These conclusions jibe with Dawn's more than two decades of experience in media law and she adds that libel plaintiffs often have an affiliation, affection or particular knowledge of law enforcement. Some are actually prosecutors, law enforcement officers, judges and attorneys, but others will show affiliations such as being members of a police benevolent league, honorary deputies or have taken courses in criminal justice.

These people are often difficult to satisfy, but you will seldom regret being gracious; you may well regret a retort made in anger.

Another delicate part of handling an unhappy subject is they often want more than a correction or clarification of the facts. They may want a personal endorsement and often the clarification or correction leaves the gist of the sting of the piece the same. Your primary goal is to be fair to your readers and striving to achieve it is a defense against a libel claim. If you keep your focus on what is fair to the readers everyone comes out ahead.

Chapter 9

Check List on Public Figures

1. **The New York Times v Sullivan is the most significant libel law ruling you should remember. It essentially said in order to libel public officials a media outlet would have to publish false information knowingly with malice.**

2. **Gertz v Welch, Inc. another key case returned development of libel law to the states to determine who is a private figure and that a person could become a public figure by thrusting himself or herself into a public controversy or achieving notoriety or lasting fame.**

3. **Be careful concluding convicted criminals are public figures. Old charges of several decades ago might not be deemed relevant.**

4. **A good test is: Is there anything in this story or column that is going to hurt someone's reputation? Then ask, "is it relevant?"**

5. **Before publishing hold the citizen up to Donna Lee Dickerson's test to determine a public figure included in this chapter.**

Chapter 9

Public Officials And Public Figures:

New York Times v Sullivan And Its Progeny

The most significant libel law ruling in the history of the United States wasn't over a Pulitzer prize winning article. It was over a full page advertisement in The New York Times, headlined, "Heed Their Rising Voices," protesting a wave of violence in the South against blacks involved in civil rights demonstrations. L. B. Sullivan a Montgomery, Alabama police commissioner said he was libeled by some of the claims in the ad and it turned out there were some inaccuracies. For example the punished black students in one instance sang "The Star Spangled Banner" not "My Country Tis of Thee." Nine students were expelled, not for leading a demonstration, but for insisting on service at a county courthouse lunch counter and police, while deployed nearby, never ringed the campus as the ad claimed. The jury found sufficient other error to find The Times guilty and returned a verdict for $500,000. This was affirmed by the Alabama Supreme Court and appealed to the U.S. Supreme Court.

In **New York Times v Sullivan, 376 US 254; 84 S Ct 710; 11 L Ed 2d 686 (1964)** the U.S. Supreme Court for the first time tied defamation law to the First Amendment and created a new era in American journalism. The Sullivan decision meant the plaintiff had to show a newspaper had published significant false information and published it knowingly or recklessly. In other words, had exhibited "actual malice."

In effect Sullivan made most public officials libel proof and subsequent court rulings have tried to discriminate among public officials, public figures, public employees and private citizens. Subsequent decisions have held publishers accountable for reckless falsity. For example, if a charge about a public officials were so outrageous that the publisher suspected its truth then he might be accountable should he print it without checking the claim.

Most journalists have heard of Sullivan even though they didn't know it was over an advertisement. Another key case in the development of current libel law, the 1974 Supreme Court decision in **Gertz v Welch, Inc., 418 US 323; 94 S Ct 2997; 41 L Ed 2d 789 (1974)** is less well known. It returned the development of libel law to the states insofar as pertaining to private figures seeking recovery for defamatory statements about them. **Gertz** demonstrated a person could become a public figure by thrusting himself or herself into a public controversy or by achieving notoriety or lasting fame. Merely being a prominent attorney does not make person a public figure and the key test , according to William Francois, former head of the Wayne State

Journalism program and author of the textbook "Mass Media Law and Regulation" is voluntary action on the part of an individual in connection with a public controversy.

Are convicted criminals public figures? Before answering, yes, you should realize that the older the charge or conviction is the more likely a court is going to find it not relevant. For example, if you discover that the 75 year old winner of the Best Pie Contest was arrested and convicted of blowing up mail boxes as a teenager, you might want to ask yourself what relevance that has to her First Prize sixty years and a respected and successful career later.

The courts have also attempted to define public controversy in their efforts to determine who is a public figure. For example in the **Firestone v Time, 424 US 448; 96 S Ct 958; 47 L Ed 2d 154 (1976)** case in Florida in 1976 the courts determined that Mrs. Firestone was not a public figure even though she held press conferences to discuss reporters' questions in connection with her highly publicized divorce from the auto tire heir. The courts found there was no public controversy involved although there might have been a great deal of interest in the gossip surrounding the case.

Donna Lee Dickerson, chair of the Department of Communication at the University of South Florida at Tampa gives these clues in "Florida Media Law, " for reporters trying to decide if an individual is a public figure:

- Did the person inject himself or herself into a public issue to attempt to affect its outcome?
- Was the person heavily involved in an area of high community concern?
- Does the individual have a broad community reputation involving the activity?
- Has the person actively sought attention from the media or the public?
- Has extensive debate put the individual into the limelight?

A yes answer to any of these questions probably means the person will be considered a public figure.

Obviously the history of libel can't be covered here in the detail that your attorney might like. But you should know that libel law is not static. It is constantly changing.
A few years ago it was felt that columnists were given considerable latitude in terms of what they could and could not say. And as recently as the last couple of a years a columnist for one big Michigan newspaper told a television station executive, who complained about factual inaccuracies in the column: "I don't have to check the facts. I'm a columnist." He is a columnist who apparently is unaware of a U.S. Supreme Court ruling in 1989 in an Ohio case, **Milkovich v Lorain Journal Co, 497 US 1; 110 S Ct 2695, 111 L Ed 2d 1 (1990)** in which a sports columnist was successfully sued for saying a high school wrestling coach had lied under oath. "Draping a statement in terms of opinion doesn't dispel the factual implications contained in the statement," the court observed.

A good test for you to consider from a journalistic point of view might be: Is there anything in this story or column that is going to hurt someone's reputation? If the answer is yes, then you should start applying Ms. Dickerson's tests of whether that person is a public figure. And if you are still confused after that use the editor's ultimate answer on responsible newspapers, which you will hear from us repeatedly: "When in doubt, leave it out."

Chapter 10

Rouch Case Lessons Check List

1. **If you follow up the disposition of arrests that you print in the paper or carry on your station, it will help you avoid a Rouch situation.**

2. **Check your facts against written statements in public documents not oral statements, for maximum protection.**

3. **There are no minor errors in a crime story in the mind of an aggrieved citizen.**

4. **Don't rely solely on oral representations by police officers or other public officials.**

5. **Unless it is a story of compelling public interest, i.e. a madman, serial rapist, or the Governor has been captured, or the accused is a public official, consider not publishing the name of a person arrested until after he or she has been formally arraigned.**

6. **The Rouch case caused the media to seek an amendment to the libel statute which now allows you to use police reports, public announcements, press releases, that is to say virtually all public documents, so use them!**

Chapter 10

Lessons from the Rouch Decisions

One of the most expensive and influential stories in the history of 20th century Michigan libel law ran six paragraphs on an inside page of the Battle Creek Enquirer & News shortly before Christmas in 1979. Written by veteran reporter Stanley Kaufman, it was similar to a hundred other stories obtained by newspaper police reporters across the nation making phone checks that day.

Dubbed the Rouch case, for the name of the cereal factory worker who figured in the report, the subsequent libel suit wound its way up to the Michigan Supreme court twice and the U.S. Supreme Court once before it finally ended with a victory for the newspaper. The Rouch case had a chilling effect on how and when the media covered arrests and reported the names of those arrested and it caused the Michigan Legislature to pass a law to insure that the media would be able to report information obtained from police officers in criminal cases without threat of libel suits.

On December 21, Kaufman, who had worked three decades at the Enquirer and had broken in many young police reporters on the beat, was making routine police phone checks of outlying townships after having personally visited the State Police post and the city police department. Kaufman was well known and trusted by the officers as a reliable journeyman. When police officers know and trust a reporter they will frequently tip the writer off on stories from nearby jurisdictions. That happened on this day.

Officers in Emmett Township advised Kaufman that they had arrested a rape suspect on behalf of Bedford Township at 5:25 a.m. Bedford Township confirmed the arrest, according to Kaufman, but didn't release any information on the suspect. Later, Kaufman recalls, Emmett Township officers gave him the name of the suspect and advised him to confirm it with Bedford. Kaufman worked past his 3 p.m. quitting time to wrap up the story with Bedford and got confirmation from the county prosecutor's office who said a cereal company worker, David J. Rouch had been charged with first degree criminal sexual assault and released on $10,000 personal recognizance bond.

So Kaufman talked to his Managing Editor Danny Martin and wrote the following story, put it in the city desk basket and left. [1] The story appeared inside the Saturday newspaper:

"Police Arrest Suspect in Baby-sitter Assault"

"A 43-year-old man has been arrested and charged with the sexual assault of a 17-year-old women (sic) who was baby-sitting with his children at his ex-wife's house on North Finlay Avenue in Bedford Township.

The suspect has been identified by Bedford Township Police as David J. Rouch of 631 Golden Ave. He is free on a $10,000 personal recognizance interim bond pending his arraignment in District 10 Court next week. Rouch is charged with first-degree criminal sexual conduct.

Police said Rouch allegedly entered the house about 4 a.m. Friday and attacked the young woman. He is said to have used a knife to cut the victim's clothes off, police said.

The victim later called a relative, who took her to Community Hospital and then called police. The suspect was identified by his children, according to police.

Rouch was arrested at his home by Emmett Township police, who were informed where he lived by Bedford Township investigators.

The charge against Rouch was authorized Friday by the Calhoun County Prosecutor's Office." [2]

Aside from using "women" rather than "woman" there are inaccuracies in the story based on the information the police provided Kaufman. Rouch was identified by his step-children not his own children. Rouch was never actually charged in the legal sense. He was arrested and detained by Emmett Township officers on behalf of Bedford Township without prior authorization by the prosecutor. After Rouch arrived at the station house an officer briefed an assistant prosecutor on the complaint and the circumstances and the prosecutor authorized lodging the suspect on the sex complaint. Whether those errors were minor or worth millions were key issues in the case for the next half dozen years.

When Rouch appeared for his arraignment on December 28 he was advised that no charges would be filed and that the police had pursued another suspect. No follow up story ever appeared in the Enquirer advising that police had concluded Rouch was not their man. Another person later was arrested in the case and also never charged because of a lack of evidence.

Under Michigan law if a citizen feels libeled, he or she must file suit within a calendar year of the objectionable publication. Normally an unhappy citizen will demand a retraction and a newspaper has that year to correct its error if it believes it made one. Rouch apparently spoke to several attorneys including the prosecutor about his unhappiness with the story. He later said prankster fellow workers had left red ski masks in his lunch box and on his machinery. The attacker had worn a similar mask to conceal his identity. "It wasn't any joke to me," Rouch said in a deposition. "I just know for damn sure that I'm a conversation piece. I never was before." A prosecutor advised Rouch to contact the newspaper and almost a year later after Rouch finally demanded a retraction the paper did a follow up on the case. Even so, with the deadline looming, a complaint dated December 2 was filed by Attorney John Jereck, a veteran litigator and former prosecutor, on Mr. Rouch's behalf. Jereck charged that the story had brought Rouch into "public scandal, infamy and disgrace" that his client was "totally humiliated and disgraced". He asked for $1 million and he got it--for awhile. [3]

After 18 months of pre-trial motions. depositions and other discovery, in 1982 the Calhoun County Circuit Court granted the Enquirer's motion to dismiss the case because Rouch had failed to prove actual malice on the part of Kaufman or the Gannett owned newspaper under Michigan's common law public interest privilege.

Jereck appealed the dismissal and got a strange, but favorable ruling from an Appellate Court panel saying the Circuit Court erred and ordering a trial. The appellate panel held in September 1984 the report of the arrest of a suspect in the rape of a babysitter was not of public interest concern but "merely matters that the public would find generally interesting." They said the statutory privilege was unavailable because "no warrant was issued, that the details of the alleged crime fell outside the scope of matters promoting the public interest, and that the trial court erred in requiring a showing of malice." [4] The appellate panel added that the newspaper could have run the details of the assault without using the suspect's name or they could have named a suspect without saying why he was arrested. Newspaper editors across the state and the nation were incredulous. They saw the prospect of being able to say: "John Smith was held by police for questioning in a undisclosed matter," or "a person is being questioned in a sexual assault, but we can't tell you who."

After the favorable verdict Attorney Jereck observed: "I don't believe the rights of one person or institution exist at the expense of others, in this case David Rouch. I realize it's important to newspapers. But it's important to David Rouch. And remember, he is just one guy who does not have the money or means the media do." Jereck told Detroit Free Press reporter Joe Swickard that Rouch was the classic non-public figure, a workingman who had lived his life quietly out of the public eye. "If this were the mayor or the chief of police, I'd say yes, print his name and as soon as possible," Jereck said. "These people are public officials and their conduct should be examined closely. But why is David Rouch or Fred Smith or just anybody so important that a newspaper can't wait until it has been submitted to the Prosecutor's office? David Rouch has just as many rights as you fellows." [5]

The appellate ruling was immediately appealed to the Michigan Supreme Court which dealt with two issues: whether a report of an arrest was a "public and official proceeding" privileged under Michigan statutory law and whether the "public interest and concern" privilege applied to a report on an arrest of a suspect for the rape of a baby-sitter.

In affirming the case in 1986 and ordering it to trial, the state high court set a new negligence standard for Michigan libel law: that private citizens who sue the news media are required only to prove that a news organization acted negligently. Before that ruling, known as Rouch I, a private figure was also required to establish that the news organization acted with knowing and reckless disregard for the truth if the subject matter was of public concern. The public interest privilege in Michigan was dead. Only the public status of the person is important, the court held, not the public interest status of the topic. The court concluded that news media should be held to a higher standard in dealing with falsity for private citizens and that a trial court should review the evidence even if the subject matter was of public interest.

Newspaper editorial writers across the state spoke out against the ruling and in response, Rep. William Bryant Jr., a Grosse Pointe Republican, in 1987 introduced a **House Bill 4932** to protect news organizations from libel suits when they accurately report information obtained from police records. The bill broadened the statutory public and official proceedings privilege and codified the public official and public figure standard. [6]

Even the jurist who wrote the opinion remanding the Rouch case for trial suggested legislative action might be necessary. Justice James Brickley, a former Lieutenant Governor and FBI agent, advised the Michigan Association of Broadcasters that state laws should be changed to protect news media from libel suits when they obtain information from police blotters. [7]

The Rouch case finally went to trial in early 1988 as the first to be tried under the new negligence standard. Calhoun County Circuit Judge Stephen Miller dismissed part of the suit asking for $500,000 in punitive damages which charged the newspaper acted with common law malice. Judge Miller said there was no evidence to support the contention that the Enquirer printed the story knowing it was false.

Both sides reached out for big gun experts to bolster their causes. Jereck brought in a heavy hitter to lay blame on Kaufman and the Enquirer. Pulitzer Prize winner reporter, turned college professor, turned expert witness for plaintiffs, Clark Mollenhoff testified that Kaufman was incompetent and that the Enquirer acted too hastily in going to press with the story. He said the paper should have held the story for two or three days. He sought to characterize Kaufman as unqualified to work the police beat. Mollenhoff, a journalism professor at Virginia's Washington and Lee University, was quizzed by the newspaper's attorney and admitted he was being paid $200 an hour for his appearance as a professional witness. [8]

The Enquirer hired the director of the University of Missouri School of Journalism graduate program, a former editor at the Chicago Daily News. Roy Fisher testified: "If I were arrested . . . I would pray to God that my name would be plastered all over the front page so that (friends) would be aware of my plight." The story complied with journalistic standards of truth and accuracy, according to Fisher, "because it happened." Fisher pointed to the police report as he supported the newspaper. [9]

Kaufman testified he was uncertain who he had obtained his information from in the Bedford Township Police Department, but the Chief John Bell denied that his department had provided the material and said it was department policy to withhold such information. Bell's department had paid Rouch $4,000 in an out-of-court settlement of a lawsuit charging false arrest. [10]

After seven days of testimony and argument the six-member jury began deliberations and a day later concluded the newspaper was liable. Plaintiff's counsel Jereck suggested the jury send a message to newspapers that individual rights had to be protected with their verdict and recommended a $3.3 million judgment against the newspaper. He characterized the parent company Gannett as greedy, and as more interested in profits than in its responsibility to gather information accurately since its reporter used the telephone rather than going to the added expense and time of visiting each police station. And lest you have any doubts, this is an argument made by plaintiff's attorneys in libel cases over and over. And it is an effective argument. Newspaper attorney Robert Bernius said the newspaper did not have a crystal ball to foresee what would happen with Mr. Rouch and that no one could predict that the charges would not be filed. The jury apparently agreed with Jereck, and his original price tag. After four hours of deliberation they awarded Rouch $1 million, the largest-ever libel judgment in Michigan outside of Detroit.

Media law experts quickly warned that the verdict would impede coverage of crimes and arrests. "Anyone who thinks this doesn't have an intimidating or chilling effect on newspapers is kidding themselves," said John J. Ronayne III, who represented Detroit's Channel 4, WDIV-TV, the Associated Press and the Michigan Association of Broadcasters

Herschel Fink, an attorney and former newspaper editor, who had filed an amicus brief on behalf of his client The Detroit Free Press pointed out that "80 to 90 percent of jury libel verdicts go against the media. But 80 to 90 percent of those are reversed on appeal." [11]

Judge Stephen Miller ordered the Enquirer to post a $2.2 million bond while it appealed the verdict and refused to reduce the $1 million award. Judge Miller rejected the newspaper's argument that the story was essentially accurate. He cited the part of the story that said Rouch had been arrested and charged with first-degree criminal sexual conduct. "That I think was false. Mr. Rouch was never charged with anything. He was arrested. I'm not going to change the verdict of the jury. It is very difficult . . . if not impossible to put a money figure on a reputation." Judge Miller conceded to an Associated Press reporter that the Enquirer had raised legitimate points of dispute, but said: "I'm really not too sure how that will come out in the appellate courts. I think (Rouch) may have the best argument." [12]

Meanwhile the Legislature, pressed by the media and statistics which showed Michigan libel awards had jumped dramatically after the 1986 Michigan Supreme Court decision on Rouch, passed a version of the Bryant bill into a law that limits the extent of damages a libel plaintiff could claim as a private figure. It limited awards only to actual economic loss including attorney fees and prohibited plaintiffs from seeking exemplary damages which had played pretty much the same role as punitive damages. [13] Although this latter provision has since been weakened, a Rouch verdict is unlikely to occur.

Public Act 356 broadened the definition of what constitutes an official proceeding and effectively overruled that part of the first Rouch case. The amendment, according to Henry Saad, then a partner in the Detroit law firm of Dickinson Wright, Moon, Van Dusen & Freeman, allows reporters to publish or broadcast fair and true reports of:

1. **matters of public record.**
2. **a public and official proceeding.**
3. **governmental notice, announcement, written or recorded report.**
4. **a record journal available to the public.**
5. **an act or action of a public body.**
6. **a heading of the report which is fair and accurate.**

Saad and his associate Lisa Mikalonis pointed out that reports on matters of public interest in Michigan were now subject to the less stringent negligence standard. They predicted, "such a standard may well inhibit print and electronic media from reporting on matters of public interest because any report could now result in substantial economic damage awards if a jury finds that the media failed to meet some undefined standard of care."

"Also, almost every case may go to a jury because "negligence" is an issue for the jury and the vast majority of defamation cases that go to a jury are decided against media defendants." [14]

"Further, the unprecedented provision which allows a plaintiff to obtain attorneys' fees may encourage a significant increase in the number of libel suits filed by business against the media." [15]

On June 5, 1990 an appellate court panel voted 2-1 to uphold the verdict against the newspapers in what had come to be known as Rouch 2. Writing for the majority Janet T. Neff, said there was enough evidence for the jury to decide the article was false and that the newspaper had been careless. Dissenting Judge Glenn S. Allen Jr., said the article was accurate "except for one minor misstatement of fact" and that the newspaper had correctly reported Rouch's arrest and his status as suspect. [16]

Fink accurately predicted that ruling would also be taken to Michigan's Supreme Court for a final say. I think that the idea that a news organization can be held accountable in this case in the amount of $1 million, for what was at bottom line a substantially accurate account of a criminal investigation is highly disturbing. I think that the Rouch decision generated such confusion in Michigan libel law that I think there is the possibility that the court may revisit the whole issue of the standard of care," the former newspaper reporter and editor told the Free Press. [17]

Just over a year later the High Court agreed to review the $1 million verdict. It gave four media companies (The Detroit News, the Michigan Press Association, Booth Newspapers and Post-Newsweek, owner of WDIV-TV, Channel 4 in Detroit) permission to file briefs in support of the Enquirer's legal position that the libel claim violated the newspaper's freedom of the press under the First Amendment. At oral argument, Enquirer Attorney Robert C. Bernius said, "We're arguing there was no negligence because this article was based on what police said." Attorney Jereck responded that the suit should persuade the media to "print their articles in a fashion that wouldn't leave any question to the public on guilt or innocence." [18]

Another year passed before the Court, in a divided opinion, concluded that the errors in the newspaper report were minor and did not undermine the essential truth of the story. "Newspapers have a long-standing tradition of reporting on criminal justice and police conduct," Justice Patricia J. Boyle, writing for the majority said. "Protecting that tradition without trampling the rights of individual citizens is the task facing this court." [19]

"The sting of the article was that Rouch had been identified by persons to whom he was well-known and was charged with first-degree criminal sexual conduct. That is true," Justice Boyle wrote. "The question whether a formal warrant had been issued or an arraignment held, like the question of whether it was his children or former stepchildren who identified him, did not affect the article's substantial truth," she said.

Justices Boyle, Brickley, Robert Griffin and Conrad Mallett Jr., said it was acceptable for the newspaper to use "charge" to convey that Rouch had been accused. The plaintiff had argued that the choice of one word "charge" over another, "accused" made the newspaper liable. But the Supreme Court disagreed, "We cannot accept this as a basis for liability. To do so would totally eviscerate the "breathing space" that the Constitution requires in order to protect important First Amendment rights. When writing about criminal justice or legal matters, newspapers would be forced to recapitulate technical legal terminology . . . even when popular words might be clearer to the lay reader," Boyle said. Justice Dorothy Comstock Riley concurred in the conclusion in a separate opinion.

The justices also stressed the need for independent judicial review of all the facts in such cases to determine falsity. "We perceive an additional need for independent review grounded on the fear that juries may give short shrift to important First Amendment Rights," Boyle wrote. She acknowledged in libel actions such review "reflects an inherent distrust of allocating unlimited decisional power to juries in the First Amendment context."

The justices compared the original 10 sentence article as it read in the Enquirer and as Rouch's attorney said it should have read. (The changed words are in parenthesis. Words in capital letters are words that would be changed from the original story.)

Police arrest suspect in baby-sitter assault

A 43-year-old man has been ARRESTED AND CHARGED **(arrested and accused) with the sexual assault of a 17-year-old woman who was baby-sitting with his** CHILDREN **(ex-wife's children) at his** EX-WIFE'S **(her) house on North Finlay Avenue in Bedford township.**

The subject has been identified by Bedford Township Police as David J. Rouch of 631 Golden Avenue. He is free on a $10,000 personal recognizance interim bond pending his arraignment in District 10 Court next week. Rouch CHARGED WITH **(accused of) first degree criminal sexual conduct.**

Police said Rouch allegedly entered the house about 4 a.m. Friday and attacked the young woman. He is said to have used a knife to cut the victim's clothes off, police said.

The victim later called a relative, who took her to Community Hospital and then called police. The suspect was IDENTIFIED BY HIS CHILDREN, **(ex-wife's children) according to police.**

Rouch was arrested at his home by Emmett Township Police, who were informed where he lived by Bedford Township investigators.

The CHARGE **against Rouch** WAS AUTHORIZED FRIDAY BY THE CALHOUN COUNTY PROSECUTOR'S OFFICE. **(The Calhoun County Prosecutor's office authorized the incarceration of Rouch on allegations of criminal sexual conduct in the first degree.)**

"We cannot agree that the gist or sting of the article is changed by these minor differences," Boyle's opinion said in reversing the $1 million award. [20]

Attorney Jereck appealed the decision to the U.S. Supreme Court which on March 1, 1993 refused to review the reversal. By a 7-2 vote the highest court in the land let stand the decision that tossed out the jury award.

"Poor Mr. Rouch did nothing wrong except for getting arrested for a crime he didn't commit," Rouch's appellate attorney Frank Eaman said. "Sooner or later, they're going to have to provide protection to plaintiffs whose reputations are damaged."

In counterpoint, "This decision reaffirms the right of the press to cover police activities and recognizes that reporters must rely on police reports that are not always precisely accurate," said Robert H. Giles, editor and publisher of The Detroit News. [21]

The case that hinged on a simple word like "charged" rather than accused and one error of identification –"step-children" rather than children-- and that had taken thousands of hours of attorney, editor, reporter and judicial time and millions of dollars in costs was finally over.

Rouch had a chilling effect on Michigan newspapers most of which adopted polices of not naming suspects until they were formally charged in court. Others stopped naming suspects at all in most police stories until they were convicted. And some stopped naming suspects or victims at all so if they never followed up they wouldn't be open to question.

But in the end the Rouch II Court restored common sense to Michigan libel law. The case also reaffirmed the Michigan Supreme Court's opinion in **Locricchio v Evening News Association, 438 Mich 84; 476 NW2d 112 (1991)**, which said the justices had an obligation to review the facts in libel cases to see if juries had properly followed the law.

While Attorney Jereck made no money, but helped cause a change in the libel law, he is still bitter about the 12 years he devoted to the case.

When asked if justice was served, he said: "Absolutely not . . . There is, in my opinion, no longer in Michigan libel actions available to private persons against media defendants . . . . After 12 years they sit up there basically and said without any precedent . . . that there was now a new Constitutional level of proof that they had to review."[22] "I don't care what level of proof they reviewed, when the paper says his own children identified him. That's the mistake they made. That wasn't our mistake. It was their mistake. Then to say that we did not meet a level of proof where he is dammed by the statement, I just can't understand. I believe it was political . . .."

"It was a sad day in libel for the state of Michigan for private person plaintiffs against the media," said Jereck, who has not kept in touch with Rouch. "You may as well forget considering filing now. In my opinion, he got screwed."

Rouch, who is now in his 50's does not want to discuss the case. "I was taking cases in 1980 to make money not law. As it turned out I made law and no money," Jereck said. [23]

Because the Gannett Company, parent corporation of The Enquirer never gave up and several other media organizations joined the fight, Michigan newspapers have the ability to report cases that need to be brought to the public attention without fear of protracted litigation over minor errors. And the Michigan legislature has restored police reports to official proceeding status.

The original crime, the attack on and rape of the teenaged babysitter, was never solved.

1. Telephone interview with Stanley Kaufman, former Battle Creek Enquirer & News reporter, taped with permission, June 1995.

2. **Rouch 1**, 427 Mich at 161, 398 NW2nd at 247. See **Michigan Compiled Laws Ann. 600.2911** (West Supp. 1993).

3. "News Media going to war over libel suit ruling in rape arrest," by Joe Swickard, Detroit Free Press, Comment section, Dec. 9, 1984.

4. Michigan Supreme Court Syllabus, **Rouch** v **Enquirer & News of Battle Creek** (After Remand), Docket No. 89799, by Reporter of Decisions William F. Haggerty.

5. Ibid. "News Media going to war. ." .by Joe Swickard.

6. Detroit College of Law Review, 1994, Issue 1, Spring, "Rouch v. Enquirer & News of Battle Creek: The Michigan Supreme Court Redefines and Reinvigorates Public Interest Speech in Michigan," by Richard E. Rassel and James E. Steward and Detroit College of Law Review 1989, Issue 2, Summer, "House Bill 4932 and the Rouch Case: A Brief Sketch of Michigan Libel Law," by Rudy J. Nichols.

7. "Libel Law Changes Urged," Detroit Free Press, Aug. 7, 1987, Page 7A.

8. "Paper printed rape story too soon, educator testifies," Detroit Free Press, Feb. 11, 1988, Page 6A.

9. "Educator: Printing Arrest has value," Detroit Free Press, Feb. 18, 1988, Page 12B.

10. "Newspaper loses $1 million libel suit," Detroit Free Press, Feb. 20, 1988, Page 3.

11. "Paper Faulted for Lack of follow-up," Detroit Free Press, Feb. 21, 1988, Page 7A.

12. "Judge allows libel verdict to stand," by Katherine Rizzo, Associated Press, Detroit Free Press, April 19, 1988, Page 5A.

13. **MCL 600.2911.**

14. In fact, that has not happened. While a jury may be quick to conclude that a reporter or newspaper has been negligent, the Michigan Supreme Court established in Locricchio v. Evening News Association and reaffirmed later in Rouch II that it reserves the right to review the facts in a case to make sure juries have not erred under the law. Plaintiffs lawyers working on contingency are aware of that and do not want to invest a lot of time and money in cases that will get overturned when they reach the state high court.

15. The New Michigan Law on Libel, by Henry W. Saad and Lisa R. Mikalonis, Editor & Publisher, March 11, 1989, Page 24-25.

16. "Newspaper must pay $1 million for libel, appeals court rules," Detroit News, June 5, 1990, Page B 3.

17.. "Libel Ruling Upheld in Case Based on Arrest," by Jacquelyn Boyle, Detroit Free Press, June 6, 1990, Page 3B.

18.. "State High Court to Reconsider $1-million Verdict in Libel Suit," Detroit News, July 10, 1991, Page 2B.

19. "Court overturns $1-million libel award against newspaper," by Eric Freedman, Detroit News, July 16, 1992, Page B-1.

20.. Michigan Supreme Court Syllabus, Rouch v Enquirer & News of Battle Creek (After Remand), Docket No. 89799, Decided July 15, 1992, prepared by William F. Haggerty.

21. "U.S. high court rebuffs Rouch's appeal in libel case," by Eric Freedman, Detroit News, Mar. 2, 1993, Page 1B.

22.Actually Attorney Jereck is incorrect. **Locricchio** v **Evening News Association**, 438 Mich 84, 476 NW2nd 112 (1991) cert denied 112 S Ct 1267 (1992) established that the Court has an obligation to review the facts to determine that a plaintiff has identified a material falsity in his allegations and that a material falsity occurred. Some legal experts believe that the Locricchio case which was at trial for more than two months and dragged on from 1980 to 1991 was the most expensive libel case in Michigan legal history. The stories in question were an extensive look at the ownership of a popular outdoor entertainment complex and links with possible organized crime figures. The end result of the case was that the newspaper, the Detroit News, prevailed and the U.S. Supreme Court refused to consider an appeal.

23. Interview with Battle Creek attorney John Jereck, June 1995, taped with permission.

Chapter 11

Advertising Law Check List

1. A newspaper has no legal duty to publish advertising or letters to the editor.

2. Newspapers can and do censor advertising and turn down ads they find objectionable.

3. Newspapers can be sued for the contents of advertisements they run, but they do not warrant the products, services or results promised in the ad.

4. You should watch for obviously defamatory statements, invasions of privacy or invitations to illegal activity.

5. If the advertisement contains language that would alert a reasonable publisher to clearly identifiable risk that an advertiser were offering criminal services the media outlet could lose.

6. Government does have the right to regulate the content of "commercial" speech.

7. The laws protecting copyrights and trademarks are applicable to advertisements.

8. The government prohibits advertisements promoting discrimination in housing or employment.

9. Similarly no ads promoting lotteries or raffles other than those authorized by the state may be run.

10. Liquor law advertising has been historically banned, but a 1996 U.S. Supreme Court ruling has placed that law in doubt. You may not use the image of an "ex-dead President" in conjunction with liquor ads.

11. Your newspaper should have a policy on political advertisement and the advertising and editorial department should work in cooperation to make sure defamatory ads with outrageous charges do not get into print.

12. Watch for attempts to take advantage of last minute charges that an opponent can't answer. Weeklies are particularly vulnerable.

13. **You cannot charge more for political advertising than you do for similar categories. You should have the same policy for all candidates. If one must pay cash in advance then all should be treated the same way.**

14. **Cigarette advertising must carry a warning label and advertisers who say they are liquidating must be going out of business.**

15. **The price of legal advertising is set by the Legislature.**

16. **For more detailed information you should refer to the Michigan Press Association publication, "Publications Law Affecting Michigan Newspapers."**

Chapter 11

Michigan Advertising Law

Newspapers have no legal duty to publish advertising or letters to the editor. Newspapers can turn down advertising they find objectionable. When Michigan's most infamous physician was trying to get his start in the assisted suicide business a few years ago, Dr. Jack Kevorkian took advertising copy and a picture to the Daily Tribune of Royal Oak offering a crude suicide machine for sale.

When the publisher rejected the advertisement the doctor suggested his First Amendment rights to free speech were being infringed, but he was wrong. Kevorkian then went to the Detroit News with his story of Oakland publishers refusing his ads and they did a feature on him and his device and the rest is history.

For years The Detroit News under the old Evening News Association refused to run advertisements for X-rated movies and at one time The Lansing State Journal had an advertising salesman screen and censor such advertisements in terms of titles and skin exposed. The State News, the student daily at Michigan State University had no such policy and office wits liked to compare how The State Journal's copy and the student newspaper's copy differed. For example, one film "Back Door Sex," became "Unusual Approach" before it reached the Journal Lansing readers. In September 1995 a Michigan Circuit Court Judge ordered an adult book store and theater to pay attorney fees and court costs to the Muskegon Chronicle after he threw out the theater's claim that its constitutional rights were violated because the newspaper refused its ads. The judge said the suit had no legal merit.

Knight Ridder, owner of The Detroit Free Press, recently decided its individual newspapers could decide whether they wanted to run cigarette advertising, but that corporate policy was that they didn't want ads that make cigarette smoking look sexy in any of its 34 newspapers. It should be noted that cigarette advertising, once a significant revenue producer for newspapers, has mostly moved to other publications such as magazines.

The First Amendment right of free expression includes the right not to express. When a Court ordered a defendant to place an ad in a local paper to acknowledge his misconduct, the newspaper refused to run the ad. The judge was powerless to force the newspaper to run the ad.

The advertising departments at Michigan newspapers have to worry about all the same things as the news department and several additional areas. Here are some of them.

Libel, Defamation, And Privacy.

Newspapers can be sued for libelous statements or for statements which invade privacy if they are contained in advertisements. **New York Times v Sullivan, 376 US 254; 84 S Ct 710; 11 L Ed 2d 686 (1964)** was a libel suit brought over a full page advertisement in the New York Times supporting the civil rights movement in the South. Lawsuits have also been brought over ads, even classified ads, for invasion of privacy. Therefore, the advertising department needs to be as sensitive to libel and privacy concerns as the editorial department.

Discriminatory Ads: Employment And The Federal Housing Act

Michigan's Elliot-Larsen Civil Rights Act and the Federal Housing Act prohibit publishing, printing, circulating, posting or mailing statements or advertising discriminating against anyone for a job on the basis of race, sex, color, national origin, religion, age, height weight or marital status. Federal and state law also prohibits such discrimination in advertisements to rent or sell real estate except federal law does not include height and weight restrictions. An employer claiming a Bonafide Occupational Qualification (BFOQ) should get a certificate indicating the exception. Only the government can grant such an exception. For example: even though it may seem logical to an Indian tribe that they require applicants for the superintendent of their schools to be Native American, that is not the newspaper's call.

With a few exceptions examples of advertising language which have been deemed dangerous include such references as: adults, adults only, mature adults, no children/kids, no young children, kids first floor only, families preferred, married couples only, singles.

The simplest rule for housing ads is: describe the property, not the people. For example: "one-bedroom" not, suitable for couple; "near community services", not near churches. There is an exception for qualifying senior citizen housing, but again the government makes the determination and issues certificates.

Fair Housing laws are tricky and can be expensive if violated. The New York Times has been in court for several years over a charge under the federal law that the models used in housing ads favored one race over another in certain neighborhoods. The Michigan Press Association publishes a Fair Housing Manual which is helpful in discussing the many questions raised by the statue and addresses specific questions.

An ad for a roommate could specify the sex of the roommate desired under the single family dwelling exception. If you encounter a situation which is not clear The Department of Civil Rights maintains offices in Lansing, Jackson, Saginaw, Flint, Detroit, Battle Creek, Benton Harbor, Grand Rapids and Pontiac.

Under **Michigan Law, Rule 329** all real estate or related advertising by a broker much include the broker's name and telephone number or street address. An exception is made for personal property owned by a broker or associate broker.

Clearly Identifiable Risk

Newspapers and magazines can be sued for the results of advertisements other people run. While a newspaper does not have a duty to investigate every advertisement it publishes it does have a duty not to publish if the ad on its face conveys to the reader that there is a clearly identifiable, unreasonable risk that the advertiser is offering to commit a serious violent crime, including murder.

This was part of the basis for the Daily Tribune of Royal Oak rejecting that advertisement for the suicide machine which launched Dr. Jack Kevorkian's notoriety in the assisted suicide business. There being no controls over who might choose to buy such a machine and use it the publisher felt it would be irresponsible and perhaps dangerous to run the advertisement. In two suits against Soldier of Fortune Magazine the courts reached different conclusions. This advertisement in 1985 cost them a $4.75 million judgment:

> **GUN FOR HIRE: 37 year old professional mercenary desires jobs. Vietnam Veteran, discrete and very private. Body guard, courier, and other special skills. All jobs considered.**

But this ad, which resulted in a lower court jury verdict against the magazine for $9.4 million was reversed by the Fifth Circuit Court of Appeals.

> **EX-MARINES--67-69 'Nam Vets, Ex-DI, weapons specialist-jungle warfare, pilot, M.E., high risk assignments, US or overseas.**

In the first case a business partner hired the man who placed the ad to murder his partner and in the second a husband used the ad to locate a killer to murder his wife. In both cases surviving family members sued.

The Court distinguished between the two ads by saying the second "did not contain language that would alert a reasonable publisher to the clearly identifiable unreasonable risk that the advertisers were offering criminal services."

The rule is that unless an advertisement is on its face defective, a newspaper does not have liability. This means that the newspaper must watch for defamatory statements, obvious invasions of privacy, or clear invitations to illegal activity. Such ads should not be published, but absent obvious problems with an ad, the newspaper is not liable.

Thus there has been held to be no liability to the publisher for a fraudulent advertisement offering "jumbo" interest rates or for an ad which caused a reader to be injured by defective fireworks.

So if the puppy turns out not to be "housebroken" or the baby sitter left dirty dishes in the sink and ate all the pizza, the publisher is not responsible for the stained rug or the cost of the pizza. But if the puppy were advertised as a "trained killer" or if the baby sitter offers to "rid you of your children" in the ad, don't run it.

Liquor Advertising

Historically Michigan law has banned liquor advertising, but that law has been cast into doubt by a recent U.S. Supreme Court decision that struck down a 1956 Rhode Island law banning the advertisement of retail liquor prices. A majority of the high court ruled such laws do not override the First Amendment's prohibition against laws abridging freedom of speech.

"Blanket bans on commercial speech that deprive the public of accurate price information must be reviewed with 'special care' and 'rarely survive constitutional review,'" Justice John Paul Stevens said.

Michigan law specifically prohibits the use of the image of an "ex-dead President" in connection with the advertisement of liquor. One wonders how a dead President could be anything but an ex-President.

Political Advertising

Comes the season of elections and the worst appears to surface in some folks. Letters-to-the-editor are forged, advertisements contain false or distorted claims and emotions run high as name calling is frequent. There is not a lot of specific law dealing with politics and elections coverage. Michigan law requires that an ad indicate it is or is not paid for by a candidate. The law does not require an independent advertiser to list who placed the ad. However, a newspaper may formulate its own policy for the sake of its readers requiring identification of the person placing the ad. Certainly the newspaper needs such information for its bills and readers will find useful the credentials of the person supporting or opposing the candidate or ballet proposition. It is also suggested that credit to the "Committee for Better Government" is not useful. Although attributing an ad to the wrong person has some risk, as a practical matter little actual damage can be done by attributing support of a candidate to an issue nor is it likely to be defamatory. But it can be irritating and cause lots of unpleasant phone calls.

While not many law suits are won over election shenanigans it is expensive to defend a libel suit even if your attorney is confident you can eventually win it. Here is a check list for political advertising:

Elections Check List

1. Newspapers do not have to accept political ads or allow politicians access to their news columns or run letters-to-the-editor.

2. Political advertising does not have to contain an identification statement which says, "Paid for by the Mary Jones for Dogcatcher Committee", but it is not a bad idea for a newspaper to have a policy beyond that required.

3. You can't charge higher rates for political ads than you would charge other advertisers for the same space under similar conditions.

4. Watch for last minute charges designed to take advantage of your deadlines. Weekly papers with early deadlines are particularly vulnerable.

5. Check all charges with the opposing candidate. If Candidate A says Candidate B is "a known thespian" check with B and find out if he has been in a theater production recently.

6. Establish a review process for advertising copy that involves the news department. Frequently a reporter covering that race will spot a serious flaw that a sales person might miss.

7. You are allowed to editorially favor one candidate over another and run ads for one candidate and none for the other. Equal Time rules do not apply to newspapers.

Cigarette Advertising

Under federal law it is unlawful to run cigarette advertising paid for by manufacturers without a warning labels. However, remember that although your local retailer or distributor is not bound by this requirement, the ad must contain the warnings if there is coop money, i.e. money given to the retailer by the manufacturer for advertising.

The warning labels, according to the U.S. Code, Title 15 include:

SURGEON GENERAL'S WARNING: Smoking causes Lung Cancer, Heart Disease, Emphysema, And May Complicate Pregnancy.
SURGEON GENERAL'S WARNING: Quitting Smoking Now Greatly Reduces Serious Risks to Your Health.
SURGEON GENERAL'S WARNING: Smoking by Pregnant Women May Result in Fetal Injury, Premature Birth, And Low Birth Weight.
SURGEON GENERAL'S WARNING: Cigarette Smoke Contains Carbon Monoxide.

There are also specific rules on advertising lotteries and raffles and advertisements for going-out-of-business sales and liquidation sale advertising. You should check the Michigan Press Manual before accepting ads in these categories.

Legal Advertising

The maximum cost of legal advertising in Michigan for items required by statute, administrative rule, charter or court order is determined by law. Notices that governmental agencies voluntarily run are not covered. You may charge less.

Some newspapers make up the difference in cost between state set rates and their normal advertising rates by charging that amount for required affidavits.

Lotteries

Michigan law prohibits advertising lotteries other than the Michigan lottery. Many advertisers will come up with a scheme for attracting customers which constitutes a lottery as defined under Michigan law. Such schemes are illegal except in certain licensed situations for charitable organizations and it is against the law to advertise such schemes. The basic elements of a lottery are chance, consideration and prize. Thus advertising the sale of $1 tickets (consideration) for the chance to have your name drawn as the winner of a prize is illegal. Unfortunately consideration is defined as anything of value and has been held to include time spent going to a store to pick up an entry form or dropping off an entry form or placing a stamp on the entry form. Elimination of any one of the three elements prevents the scheme from being a lottery. The two easiest way to escape the designation of lottery are to require some exercise of skill such as answering a question correctly, guessing the number of beans in the jar and the like, or eliminating consideration by allowing folks to enter the contest by telephone, walk in, mail in or faxing so as to eliminate any element of consideration.

Copyright And Trademark

Advertisements are also subject to the limitations of copyright and trademark laws.

Other Advertising Regulations

There are many more regulations on advertising. For example, there are rules against running pictures of dollar bills. There are also specific rules regarding advertising bingo, child care, going out of business sales and the licensed professions. Some of the regulations place the burden on the advertiser, not on the newspaper. But an advertiser will generally appreciate a helpful pointer on the legality of an advertisement.

For a more detailed discussion you should refer to a Michigan Press Association Publication entitled, Publications Law Affecting Michigan Newspapers.

1. **Bloss v Federated Publications, 380 Mich 485, 157 NW2d 241 (1968).**

2. Presstime, Oct. 1995. P.14.

3. Stevens quote in News Media Update.

4. Publications Law Affecting Michigan Newspapers, Michigan Press Association.

Chapter 12

Student Publications Check List

1. You do not enjoy the same freedom of expression as your commercial, professional counterparts.

2. The Hazelwood decision by the U.S. Supreme Court gave school administrators greater authority to censor and control school sponsored publications.

3. You should try logic and reason with high school administrators in pursuit of your point.

4. Do not attempt to sneak something by an advisor or administrator; you will damage the chances of future editors to do good journalism.

5. You should have a copy of a book called "Law of the Student Press" published by the Student Press Law Center in your newsroom. If you have a problem call them at: 703-807-1904.

6. Be particularly careful with articles on: faculty performance, disciplinary records, letters to the editor, sex, pregnancy, death, suicide and what could be offensive advertising. Satire and parody are particularly difficult for school administrations to understand.

7. If you receive a subpoena you should accept it and contact your advisor and the Student Press Law Center, 1101 Wilson Blvd., Suite 1910, Arlington, VA 22209-2248.

8. Your advisor should subscribe to their Student Press Law Report which costs $15 per year.

Chapter 12

Michigan Student Press Law

The most damaging case against freedom of expression in high school newspapers was the U.S. Supreme Court's 1988 decision in **Hazelwood School District v Kuhlmeier, 484 US 260; 108 S Ct 562 (1988)** usually referred to in journalistic shorthand as the Hazelwood decision. Until Hazelwood the operative case on freedom of student publications was one labeled "the black arm band case," or more formally called **Tinker v Des Moines Independent Community School District, 393 US 503; 89 S Ct 733 (1969)**. The court in that 1960's decision said "students don't give up their right to freedom of expression at the schoolhouse gate." While it didn't relate directly to publications educational and legal scholars interpreted it as giving students the right to make their own decisions about content.[1]

The **Hazelwood** decision gave school administrators greater authority to censor and control school-sponsored student publications. The court concluded because Spectrum a student newspaper near St. Louis, Mo., was produced as part of a journalism class it was not entitled to strong first amendment protection and that school officials as long as they had "substantial and reasonable basis" could decide what ran and didn't run in the newspaper.[2]

What the court said exactly in **Hazelwood** was: "We hold that educators do not offend the First Amendment by exercising editorial control over the style and content of student speech in school-sponsored expressive activities so long as their actions are reasonably related to legitimate pedagogical concerns."

Attempts in Michigan to pass legislation which would take editorial control from school administrations and put it in the hands of accredited high school journalism advisors have failed. In part they failed because they did not get the support of the professional journalistic community.

While some journalists spoke out strongly in favor of such protection others pointed out that professional editors and writers get censored by their publishers from time to time and that as long as the school was paying for the production and publication of the magazine or newspaper then it was in effect the publisher. In addition the editorial voices of Michigan newspapers have been largely silent in supporting student journalists in publication of controversial subjects.

---

[1]The Detroit News, "Anchor Bay students cry foul over censorship attempt," Jan. 10, 1996.

[2]"Student Freedom of Expression and High School journalism Advisers: A Legal and Educational Dilemma," by Mary Peterson of Journalism and Mass Communication, The University of Iowa, a paper presented at the Association for Education in Journal Communication, Washington, D.C., August 1995.

When the Grosse Pointe South High School Magazine Imprints lost its funding from a parents club because it printed several pieces on student suicides and other mildly controversial articles few voices were raised on its behalf. Similarly early in 1996 there was not strong professional support for the editor of the Anchor Bay Times when Mish Charles caused an uproar among parents and administrators by writing an editorial criticizing the school's decision to repair its gym during the girls' basketball season. Ms. Charles questioned whether the same repairs and disruptions would have occurred during the boys' season.

While some school districts nationwide took steps in the seven years since Hazelwood to clarify that the student publications should enjoy First Amendment protections there is little evidence that many Michigan districts have followed suit. Dade County, Florida's draft language, considered a model for other schools states: "The Dade County school board recognizes that an unfettered student press is essential in establishing and maintaining an atmosphere of open discussion, intellectual exchange and freedom of expression on campus. It is therefore the policy of the Dade County school Board that student journalists shall be afforded protection against censorship." The language reportedly also includes the phrase: "no prior review," which student journalists feel is essential to a truly free student press.

Nationally, according to a 1995 report by a Temple University Communication Professor most student newspapers have written ethics codes which are modeled after professional ethics codes. Ironically, he reported that student newspaper advisors feel that strict adherence to the policies are more important than their professional brethren because the advisers surveyed saw loss of press freedom as a real sanction for failure to practice good journalism.[3] There are no statistics on how many Michigan high school and college newspapers have written ethics policies. But among professional newspapers nationally statistics show that less than half profess to have such codes.

Six states have taken legislative action deemed "anti-Hazelwood bills". They include Arkansas, California, Colorado, Iowa, Kansas and Massachusetts. Each of these laws essentially prohibit school officials from censoring a student publication unless the content falls into one or more categories of "unprotected speech," material that is: obscene as to minors, libelous, invasive of an individual's privacy or substantially disruptive of normal school activities.[4]

The Bible for student journalists and their advisers on their legal rights is a book called "Law of the Student Press," published by the Student Press Law Center, 1101 Wilson Boulevard, Suite 1910, Arlington, VA 22209-2248. If you are involved in working with student publications

---

[3] **Research paper presented to The Scholastic Journalism Division of Association for Education in journalism and Mass Communication annual convention, August 1995, Washington, D.C. "The High School Ethics Challenge: using Standards of Professional Journalism Without the Freedoms of the Professional Press", by Thomas Eveslage, Professor of Communication, Department of Journalism, Temple University, Philadelphia, PA.**

[4] **Scholastic Source, AEJMC Scholastic Journalism Division, July 1995, "New Arkansas law protects press freedoms for students."**

you should read it and the Center's three times a year "Student Press Law Report" The book costs $15 and a subscription to the Report costs $15. And if you have a legal question or problem relating to your rights as a student journalist or faculty advisor you can call the Center at (703) 807 1904.

For example in its Winter 1995-96 issue the Report lists seven public records high school journalists might want to get their hands on: cafeteria health reviews, school bus safety reports, building inspections, school budget information, accreditation reports, academic performance and crime statistics. It then gives a general advisory on how to obtain most of them with the caveat that laws vary from state to state and private schools may not be held to the same standards.

It should also be noted that the areas in which student journalists are likely to get into trouble with nervous administrations are roughly the same with the addition of: sports, death, race, sex, pregnancy, political correctness, drugs, corruption, abortion, satire and parody. Satire and parody are particularly in need of editorial care in editorials, cartoons and columns. If you are going to address those subjects plan your strategy carefully and make sure you got your facts right.

Another area to be careful about is advertising. In Allegan a proposed advertisement for planned Parenthood in a school yearbook sparked weeks of debate about who should decide what advertisements are acceptable in the annual before the school board decided to let students continue to make those calls. Other school districts have allowed principals to censor ads which are considered controversial. One thing school administrators prone to censorship should consider is that it is pretty easy these days to produce a school newspaper on a home computer setup. If the students feel their freedoms are being abridged they are likely to go underground and publish off campus. Again in Allegan three high schoolers started a newspaper called Foneticalli. The Allegan principal characterized the newspaper as "trash" saying it was filled with profanity and hurtful things. For example they ran a picture of one Allegan student and referred to him as a "pee-pee head" for his bullying behavior.[5]

Mark Goodman, executive director of the Student Press Law Center compiled this list of the top 10 problems confronting student journalists:

1. Subpoenas for reporter notes or photographer negatives.
2. Faculty performance articles.
3. Alcohol advertising
4. Getting locked out of covering the student government association.
5. Speech codes that prohibit offensive speech.
6. Censorship through funding.
7. Campus Crime reports.

---

[5]The Allegan County News, January 25, 1996.

8. Disciplinary records.
9. Letters to the editor can get you into libel trouble.
10. Theft of papers.

High School newspaper advisers range from well trained and committed to those who get assigned to the role reluctantly and don't even know what the First Amendment states. Most of them do not have professional journalistic training, according to a study by Mary Peterson Arnold.[6]

Perhaps the best study of high school press freedoms and the case for a free student press is made in a book by The Freedom Forum, entitled "Death by Cheeseburger, High School Journalism in the 1990's and Beyond." Complimentary copies are available from the Forum at 1101 Wilson Blvd., Arlington, VA 22209.

That book's odd title derives from a 1971 incident in a Henderson, N.C. high school. "The school newspaper was shut down that fall based on three student articles. One, 'Death By A Cheeseburger,' was a satirical tale of the death of the writer after eating a cafeteria cheeseburger. The newspaper was closed, the adviser let go, a novice hired to teach English and journalism--without the student paper."[7]

And anyone who has ever eaten a cheeseburger in a high school cafeteria should know that students ought to have the freedom to express their opinions about the food in print.

---

[6] "Student Freedom of Expression and High School Journalism Advisers: A Legal and Educational Dilemma," by Mary Peterson Arnold, School of Journalism and Mass Communication, The University of Iowa, a paper presented to AEJMC, Washington, 1995.

[7] "Death by Cheeseburger, High School Journalism in the 1990's and Beyond," a publication of the Freedom Forum, 1994, Arlington, VA.

Appendix 1

Freedom of Information Act Request

Sample Letter

(Date)	July 4, 2000
(Agency Head)	Ms. Jane Mayor
(Title)	Township Supervisor
(Location)	Harriedperson Twp.
(Address)	69 Last Hope Road
	Mukillteo, MI. 5800

Re: Freedom of Information Request

Dear Ms. Mayor

This is a request for information under the Michigan Freedom of Information Act (**MCLA 15.231** et seq.) (for Federal requests it would be **5 U.S.C. §552)**

I am requesting the following information as permitted by law. (Now detail as specifically as possible the records or information you are seeking.) You have five business days under Michigan law to either provide copies of the records or a detailed explanation why the records will not be disclosed. Since this is a matter of public interest we would request that you waive any fees. Absent that please advise me of what the fees specifically are according to statutory guidelines. (There is no five day provision under federal law, but if you are dealing with a FOI officer and he or she rejects your request you can appeal it to the agency head.)

If you need to reach me my telephone number is (000-000-0000).

Thank you in advance for your cooperation in providing information of interest to Michigan's citizens.

Sincerely,

Janis Doe, Reporter
The Mukillteo Record
20 W. Main
Mukillteo, MI 58000

Appendix 2

Sample objection to closed meeting.

I would like to be heard on the issue of closing this meeting. I am a [reporter] with [The Daily Bugle]. It is my purpose in being here tonight to cover the public business conducted at this meeting. The Michigan Open Meetings Act requires that all decisions be made a meeting open to the public and that all deliberations leading to decisions be conducted in a meeting open to the public unless the meeting is one of those in Section 8 of the Act. Listening here tonight it does not appear to me that the proceedings you intend to close are entitled to be closed under the Act. I remind you that if you meet in closed session you can have your decisions declared invalid.

I respectfully request that you delay the closed portion of this meeting until you can review this and until we can have our attorneys review this matter with you.

Appendix 3

Sample protest of closure of court.

Your Honor, may I please address the Court. I am a [reporter] with the [Daily Bugle]. My newspaper believes that the proceedings in this court are newsworthy. It is my understanding that under the constitution, Court Rules and statutes, I have a constitutional right of access to these proceedings subject to some narrow limitations. Pursuant to these rights, I ask that these proceedings not be closed.

If you intend to close these proceedings, would you please adjourn these proceedings so that I may contact our lawyer and request the filing of a motion and the opportunity to be heard on this issue of closure of the proceedings in this court.

Appendix 4

The Troy Case

Two Troy police officers mistakenly shot and killed the owner of a van parked in his own driveway, believing him to be a criminal in the process of stealing from it or vandalizing it. The police department refused to release the officers names to media citing an ongoing investigation into the incident. Reporters felt that if the men had not been police officers the City of Troy would have released their names.

The Detroit News filed a Freedom of Information request for the officers names saying they were public record. Troy officials opposed the release of the names claiming it would "interfere with law enforcement proceedings".

The case eventually wound up before the Michigan Supreme Court as **Evening News Association** v **City of Troy**, 417 Mich 481; 339 NW2d 421 (1983). The decision is one of the most important decisions to be rendered by the court with regard to FOIA. No journalist should make a FOIA request without reading it.

In construing the "interfere with law enforcement proceedings exemption," the Court noted that the defendant had only put forth generic assertions that disclosure would harm its investigation, and no particularized evidence existed in the record that disclosure of the reports would have interfered with the investigation. 417 Mich at 486. (339 NW2d at 431). Analyzing the testimony from various law-enforcement officials at the trial court hearing on plaintiff's request, the Evening News Court noted that criticism of the officers, or an attempt to protect their reputation should an internal investigation exonerate them, was not sufficient reason for withholding the material.

> Critical public reaction is not interference with law enforcement proceedings....Furthermore, public praise and criticism is part of the democratic process that FOIA seeks to promote. 417 Mich at 512. (339 NW2d at 436)

This is a quote that every reporter should carry on a card in his pocket.

The Court held that trial courts faced with a defendant asserting this exemption should follow one of three courses: either demand a particularized justification for the claimed exemptions, conduct an in camera hearing to determine whether such justifications exist, or grant plaintiff's counsel in camera access to the documents under special agreement. **Haskins** v **Oronoko Twp Supervisor**, 172 Mich App 73; 431 NW2d 210 (1988).

The Supreme Court set down the following standard for analyzing a claim of exemption from FOIA disclosure:

1. The burden of proof is on the party claiming exemption from disclosure, i.e. the public body.

2. Exemptions must be interpreted narrowly.

3. The public body shall separate the exempt and nonexempt material and make the nonexempt material available for examination and copying. **MCL § 15.244(1); MSA § 4.1801(14)(1);**

4. Detailed affidavits describing the matters withheld must be supplied by the agency.

5. Justification of exemption must be more than "conclusory," i.e. simple repetition of statutory language. A bill of particulars is in order. Justification must indicate factually how a particular document, or category of documents, interferes with law enforcement proceedings.

6. The mere showing of a direct relationship between records sought and an investigation is inadequate.

Evening News Association, 417 Mich at 502; see also **Nicita v Detroit, 194 Mich App 657; 487 NW2d 814 (1992).**

Generic denials thus do not satisfy the FOIA.

The high court concluded:

"A general claim that records are involved in an ongoing criminal investigation and that their disclosure would "interfere with law enforcement proceedings" is not sufficient to sustain an exemption under FOIA Article 13 (1)(b). A public body must indicate factually and in detail how a particular document or category of documents satisfies the exemption; mere conclusory allegations are not sufficient."

The City of Troy was ordered to pay $40,000 to the Evening News Association to cover its legal costs in pursuing the matter.

Appendix 5

Dangerous Words

Here are some of the words to watch as a reporter and editor. There are others, but these are some of the most frequently used danger words. Some are dangerous because they have specific legal meaning and short of an arraignment or conviction should not be used. Others are defamatory. It doesn't mean don't ever use them. It just means to paraphrase Dr. Seuss: Say what you mean and mean what you say. For a visit to court won't make your day.

Addict
AIDS victim
Arson
Assault
Bad Checks
Bankrupt
Bigamist
Bilk
B-Girl
Breaking and Entering
Bribery
Charge
Cheat
Criminal Sexual conduct
Drunk Driving
Ex-Convict
Embezzlement
Failure
Forge
Forgery
Gangster
Gambler
Hack
Hooker
Incompetent
Loan Shark
Loose
Mafia
Manslaughter
Mobster
Molestation
Murder

Pervert
Pimp
Prostitute
Scam
Sexual Misconduct
Shoplifter
Shyster
Steal
Streetwalker
Swindle
Swindler
Quack
Thief
Wino

And while not necessarily dangerous most news organizations ban the use of George Carlin's dirty seven unless a supervising manager specifically clears such a word because of a direct quote: The controversial words Carlin used in a 1973 radio broadcast entitled "The Seven Words You Can't Say on Radio and Television" are: shit, piss, fuck, cunt, cocksucker, motherfucker and tits.

Appendix 6

Useful Sources to Help With Questions

Federal Freedom of Information Act

FOIA contacts at Federal Agencies--October 1996 Quill .... Pages 59-63
Also contains state-by-state access numbers and contacts and
similar numbers for interested media, citizen and trade groups .... Pages 71 to 76
Office of Information and Privacy FOIA Counselor Service (202) 514-3642
Attorneys available to respond to FOI related inquiries for list of
federal FOI officers .... www.usdog.gov
Reporters Committee for Freedom of the Press .... (703) 807- 2100 - www.rcfp.org/rcfp
assistance to journalists having trouble accessing information
Radio-TV News Directors Association .... (202) 659-6510 - www.rtnda.org/rtnda/
defends rights of broadcast journalists to access news
Society of Professional Journalists .... (317) 633- 9385 - town.hall.org/places/spj/
coordinates legal defense fund and works
with First Amendment legal counsel in Washington

FOIA on Internet (From Quill Magazine List)

Legal information institute, Cornell Law School--comprehensive
archive on legal issues .... http://www.law.cornell.edu/apa/apa.table.html
Professor Barbara Croll Fought of the Newhouse School
at Syracuse University, formerly with Eastern Michigan
University, compiles an exhaustive
list of FOI resources .... http://town.hall.org/places/spj/foi-resources. html
Step-by-Step Guide to Using the Freedom of Information Act
by Allan Robert Adler, a publication of the American Civil Liberties
Union Foundation. Quill says perhaps best site for first time users.
It has sample letters
to send gopher://gopher.nyc.pipeline.com:6601/00/publications/reports/foia

Investigative Reporting

Center for Investigative Reporting Inc. .... (202) 546-1880
Investigative Reporters and Editors .... (573) 882- 4856 - www.ire.org

Michigan Freedom of Information Act

Michigan Attorney General's office .... (517) 373-1110

Michigan Freedom of Information Committee
195 Manoogian Hall
Wayne State University Detroit 48202
Information hotline .... (313) 577-8379

Michigan Press Association information hotline .... (800) 334-5390

Michigan Association of Broadcasters .... (517) 484-7444

State Bar of Michigan .... (800) 882- 6722

Society of Professional Journalists
State Sunshine Chair, Christine Uthoff .... (517) 487- 8888

Student Press Law

Student Press Law Center .... (703) 807-1904 - www.splc.org
protects First Amendment rights of high school
and college student journalists

Appendix 7

Legalese

Here is a list of legal and court terms you should know. Most are excerpted and abbreviated from the State Bar of Michigan's "A Layman's Guide to: Legal Terms." You can obtain copies of the useful booklet for 65 cents from the State Bar at 306 Townsend Street, Lansing, MI 48933-2083. Others have been added by the authors.

A

Abstract of record--An abbreviated but complete history of a case.
Amicus curiae--A "friend of the court" usually one not involved in a lawsuit who volunteers to intervene to provide information about a point of law to assist the court.
Arraignment--In criminal practice, to bring the prisoner to court in person to answer a charge.

B

Bail--Cash or other security placed on deposit with the court to obtain the release of an arrested person and to guarantee his or her appearance before the court.
Bench Warrant--An order issued by the court, (from the bench) for the arrest of a person.
Bind Over--Hold for trial.
Brief--A written argument submitted to the court by counsel setting forth the facts and the legal argument of a client's case.
Burden of Proof--The plaintiff in a personal injury lawsuit has the burden of proving that an injury occurred and the defendant caused it.
Burglary--The breaking into and entering of a building in order to commit inside it a serious crime, i.e., robbery.

C

Certiorari--An order commanding judges or officers of a lower court to certify the record of a case for judicial review by an appellate court.
Chambers--the private offices or rooms of a judge.
Change of Venue--The removal of a suit started in one county or district to another location for trial, usually on the grounds that one party cannot obtain a fair trial in the original jurisdiction and frequently caused by pre-trial publicity.
Common law--law which derives its authority from ancient usage rather than the Constitution, statutes or written rules. It is law developed by judges in opinions.
Concurrent sentences--Sentences for separate crimes which run at the same rather than consecutively.
Corpus Delicti--The object or thing upon which a crime has been committed, i.e., the body of a murdered person, the charred shell of a house.

Criminal Sexual Conduct - a term describing criminal conduct in Michigan involving intimate acts from first degree (what is historically known as rape) to fourth degree (inappropriate touching).

D

De Novo--Anew. afresh. A "trial de novo" is a retrial.
Default--A failure to do what ought to be done, i.e. when a defendant doesn't plead within the time allowed or fails to appear for trial and when an attorney fails to file required papers on a timely basis.
Deposition--Testimony of a witness given elsewhere than in open court, recorded and sworn to use at the trial.
Double Jeopardy--Being placed more than one in danger of being convicted and sentenced for the same offense.
Due process--The fundamental rules which guarantee "fair play" in the conduct of legal proceedings; i.e., the right to an impartial judge and jury, the right to present evidence on one's own behalf, the right to confront one's accuser, the right to be represented by counsel.

E

Embezzlement--The wrongful taking of property of money by a person to whom it has been entrusted.
Ex post facto--After the fact.

F

Felony--A serious crime, generally punishable by imprisonment in a state prison for more than a year.
Fraud--The intentional perversion of truth to deprive another of property or to induce a person to surrender a legal right, or to injure him or her in some other way.

G

Garnishment--A proceeding whereby a debtor's money or property held by a third party such as an employer are attached and applied to the debt.
Grand Jury--A jury of inquiry which receives complaints and accusations in criminal cases. It hears the prosecutor's evidence and issues indictments when satisfied that there is probable cause to believe that a crime was committed, that the accused committed the crime and that a trial should be held.

H

Habeas Corpus--The name of a writ used to bring a person before a court or judge. It usually commands officials to produce a detained person in court to determine if she or he is being lawfully held.
Hearsay--Second-hand evidence not arising from personal knowledge of a witness, but from what they have hard others say.

I

Indictment--A grand jury's written accusation that charges a named party with the commission of a crime.
Injunction--A court order prohibiting a threatened or continuing act.
Interrogatories--Written questions posed by one party and served on another which must be answered in writing under oath.

L

Libel--Injury to a person's character or reputation through print, writing, pictures or signs, as distinguished from the spoken word. Generally any publication that injures someone's reputation.
Lien--A claim against property to secure a debt or other obligation. A sub-contractor may hold a lien on your new house until the builder pays him off.

M

Malfeasance--The commission of an unlawful act.
Mandamus--An action seeking a court order commanding a person, corporation, public office-holder or inferior court to perform a specific act alleged to be required as part of his or its official duties.
Manslaughter--The unlawful killing of another without intent to kill.
Misdemeanor--Offenses less serious than felonies; generally punishable by fine or imprisonment in local jails.
Misfeasance--The improper performance of a lawful act.
Moot--not relevant to the court making a decision.
Moral turpitude--Conduct inherently unethical or immoral as distinguished from conduct which would be proper except for a statute which prohibits it.
Murder--The unlawful killing of a human being by another with malice aforethought. Murder in the first degree is characterized by premeditation; murder in the second degree is characterized by a sudden and instantaneous intent to kill or cause injury without caring whether it kills or not.

N

Nolo Contendere, No contest -- "I will not contest it" --a plea by a defendant in a criminal case on which, like a plea of guilty, a conviction may be entered, but unlike a guilty pea, may not be used as an admission in any other matter.
Nonfeasance--Failure to perform a lawfully required duty of a particular office.

O

Of counsel--Describes counsel hired to help prepare, manage or appeal a case, but who is not the principal attorney of record for the client.

P

Parole--Conditional release from prison before the end of a sentence; if the parolee observes the conditions, he or she need not serve the rest of the term.
Plaintiff--A person who brings a civil action; the complainant.
Probable cause--A reasonable ground, established after investigation for believing the facts warrant further proceedings.
Prejudicial Error--"Reversible error"; an error in the course of a trial serious enough to require an appeals court to reverse the judgment.
Probate--The act or process of proving the validity of a will.

Q

Quid pro quo--Something for something; a fair return; the giving of one valuable thing or service for another.

R

Reasonable doubt--An accused person is entitled to acquittal if, in the minds of the jurors, guilt is not proved beyond a "reasonable doubt"; proof beyond a reasonable doubt is that which excludes every reasonable theory of the facts except that which it tends to support, which establishes the facts to a moral certainty but not beyond all possible or imaginary doubt.
Res judicata (ras)--A claim or controversy which has been decided in court. A matter finally decided on its merits cannot again be brought before a court.

S

Sequestration of witnesses--A court order requiring each witness stay outside the courtroom until called to testify; to prevent testimony of any witness from being influenced by another.
Slander--Injury To a person's character or reputation through the spoken word rather than through print, writings, broadcasts, pictures or signs.

Statute of limitation--A statutory time limit on the right to seek relief in court for damages; providing that any claim for relief shall be barred unless begun within a specific period of time following the alleged wrong.
Stipulation--An agreement between opposing attorneys on a matter. For example, to admit certain facts or agree that a person may serve as an expert witness.
Subpoena--An order commanding a witness to appear and testify.
Subpoena Duces Tecum---An order commanding a witness to produce certain documents or records.
Summons--A writ directing a sheriff or other officer to notify the person named in the summons that an action has been started against him or her in court and that he or she is required to appear to answer the complaint.

T

Tort--An injury or wrong committed against the person or property of another, arising out of violation of a duty established by law rather than by contract.
Transcript--The record of proceedings in a trial or hearing
True bill--In criminal practice, the written endorsement made by a grand jury on a proposed indictment in which they have found sufficient evidence to warrant the issuance of an indictment.

V

Venire--Technically a writ summoning prospective jurors; popularly refers to the group of jurors summoned.
Venue--the country, city or other locality which has jurisdiction over a case.
Voir Dire-- "To speak the truth"; the preliminary examination into the qualifications of prospective witnesses or jurors.

W

Waive--To abandon or surrender a claim, privilege or right.
Waiver of immunity--A means authorized by statute by which a witness, before testifying or producing evidence, may relinquish the right to refuse to testify against himself, making it possible for the testimony to be used against him in future proceedings.
Warrant--An order issued by a magistrate, justice or other competent authority to a peace officer requiring the arrest of the person named therein.
With prejudice--Applied to orders of judgment dismissing a case, meaning the plaintiff is barred from ever bringing a lawsuit on the same claim or cause.
Without prejudice--A claim or cause dismissed which could be the subject of a new lawsuit.
Writ--A court order requiring the performance of a specific act, or which gives authority to have it done.

Appendix 8

Copyright

A copyright protects the expression of ideas. The claimant, who may be the author, has the following rights:

- To reproduce the copyrighted work in copies;
- To prepare derivative works based upon the copyrighted work;
- To distribute copies of the copyrighted work to the public by sale or other transfer of ownership, or by rental, lease or lending;
- To display the copyrighted work publicly in the case of literary works and pictorial, or graphical works.

The legally sufficient copyright notice consists of three elements:

1) placing a "c" in a circle, or the abbreviation "copr.", or the word copyright,
2) followed by the year of creation
3) together with the name of the entity or person claiming the copyright. e.g. Copyright 1994, Michigan Press Association; Copr. 1994, Michigan Press Association;

Although there is a recognized copyright by simply publishing material, it is better to use the copyright symbol. The copyright symbol puts the readers on notice that you claim a copyright. Secondly, it entitles you to seek statutory damages, including actual attorney fees once you register the copyright and in appropriate circumstances. Real monetary loss is often very hard or impossible to prove when someone lifts material from your newspaper. It may take years of copyright violations before you could show or even sustain damages that would justify going to court.

Inclusion of the copyright symbol will protect material and the format in which you place the material in the newspaper. However, it does not give you superior rights to someone who holds a copyright to a particular portion of the newspaper. If a customer places a copyrighted advertisement into your newspaper, your additional copyright symbol will protect the particular version of the copyright appearing in your paper. But it does **not** give you the right to republish the copyrighted advertisement without permission of the holder of the copyright for the advertisement.

As to editorial content and advertisements produced by you, you will have copyright protection by placing the symbol in the newspaper.

In order to prosecute for a copyright violation, the particular edition of the newspaper which was copied without permission must be registered with the copyright office by filing a copy of Application Form SE. Because the copyright office does not have room for all of the editions of your newspaper, not to mention the other 290 members of Michigan Press Association, you are only required to file this form when you need to register the work. You only need to register the work if you intend to enforce the copyright. Thus, you only need to register an edition of your newspaper when you intend to pursue your rights for a copyright violation. You must register the work within 3 months of publication of the work or prior to an infringement of the work to seek statutory damages and attorney fees. Otherwise only an award of actual damages and profits can be sought.

The advantage of registration is that it allows you to sue for statutory damages. It is often difficult to establish actual damages. But if you use the copyright symbol which is deemed to put the world on notice of your claim of copyright, you need not show actual loss. Instead you can ask the judge to award damages of at least $250 but not to exceed $50,000.

The presumption is that the work produced by employees of a newspaper belongs to the newspaper. There is a doctrine called "work for hire" which places the presumption of copyright in the employer. So art work out of your art department or by your layout person or work done by a full time reporter belongs to the newspaper. But if the person is an independent contractor, e.g. a stringer or a freelance artist, the presumption is that the independent contractor holds the copyright and you need their approval for every insertion of the material. This is true even if they did not put a copyright symbol on their work.

The corollary is that one does not use copyrighted material without specific approval of the holder of the copyright. Having said that, of course, there is an exception.

The copyright laws recognize an exception to the copyright rule for "fair use" of copyrighted materials. To determine whether or not the use of the copyrighted materials is fair use the statute provides for the following consideration:

a. the purpose and character of the use, including whether such use is of a commercial nature or is for nonprofit educational purposes;

b. the nature of the copyrighted work;

c. the amount and substantiality of the portion used in relation to the copyrighted work as a whole and

d. the effect of the use upon the potential market for or value of the copyrighted work.

For example, a book review may quote from the copyrighted book because there is attribution of any ideas or quotes taken from the book. The same is true of movie reviews.

There has been a fair bit of litigation over the scope of the fair use exemption. Thus, cavalier use of this exemption is to be discouraged.

Appendix 9

Photographing Dead Bodies

It is a felony in Michigan to photograph or publicly display a photograph of all or a portion of a dead body in a grave. A grave is defined as any site intended for the permanent internment of all or a portion of a decedent and includes the bottomlands of the Great Lakes that contain all or a portion of a decedent who died in a disaster from which it is impracticable or not intended to remove the remains.

The genesis of this legislation is not Princes Diana, having been enacted in July of this year. Rather the legislation resulted from the efforts of a photography crew to produce a documentary on the shipwreck of the Edmund Fitzgerald, a merchant ship lost in the Lake Superior some twenty years ago. All 29 people aboard were lost in this shipwreck made famous in song.

By using a submersible, divers were able to withstand the cold and the depths of Lake Superior. The photographs they took included brief images of the mostly decomposed remains of a portion of the crew. No crew member was recognizable.

Nonetheless a group of relatives of the Fitzgerald crew charged the divers were insensitive and exploited the tragedy for commercial gain. Like the public reaction to the death of Princess Diana, there is concern in Michigan that such statutes, enacted out of emotion rather than carefully thought out identification of a legitimate government interest and the proper response thereto, eviscerates public access to newsworthy events. Concern has been expressed as to the application of the statute to Holocaust Exhibits. Do such exhibits fall within the exceptions for archaeological or scientific exhibits?

Another disturbing aspect of the legislation is that it recognizes a right in the image of a decedent. Both privacy and libel claims terminate upon death of the claimant. Here there is the creation of a right in the images of a dead person.

The right seems to repose with the relatives of the decedent since the statute exempts photographs obtained with the written consent of the decedent's next of kin. The statute also exempts public displays of photographs for law enforcement, medical, archaeological or scientific purposes.

The statute is found at **Michigan Compiled Laws, Sections 750.160a and 750.160b.**

Appendix 10

Open Meetings Act - Cases and Attorney General's Opinions (For update see http://www.ag.state.mi.us/)

"Public body"includes committee, subcommittee, authority, or council which is empowered by State Constitution, statute, charger, ordinance, resolution, or rule to exercise governmental or proprietary authority. **Booth Newspapers, Inc. v University of Michigan Board of Regents, 444 Mich 211; 507 NW2d 422 (1993).**

Oral opinions of an attorney are not "public records" for purposes of the Freedom of Information Act (FOIA) and cannot be used to authorize holding a closed session under the Open Meetings Act .

Consideration of consent judgment which it had entered into did not constitute consultation regarding trial or settlement strategy, and thus meeting could not be closed. **Detroit News, Inc. v City of Detroit, 185 Mich App 296, appeal denied 437 Mich 1003, (1991).**

Statements of confidential informants from prison inmates regarding another inmate's misconduct in prison were exempt from disclosure as public record under the Freedom of Information Act, based on affidavit of prison official that informants' safety would be jeopardized and prison's ability to maintain physical security would be prejudiced if identities were revealed. **Hyson v Department of Corrections, 205 Mich App 422; 521 NW2d 841 (1994).**

Foundation created by university board of regents was a "public body" under Open Meetings Act (OMA) since the foundation was empowered by resolution of the board of regents to exercise proprietary authority over university's endowment. **Jackson v Eastern Michigan University Foundation, 215 Mich App 240; 544 NW2d 737 (1996).**

Whether school board members intended to violate Open Meetings Act was irrelevant and did not preclude summary judgment where opposing party was seeking only injunctive relief and did not request civil damages. **Meyers v Patchkowski, 216 Mich App 513; 549 NW2d 602 (1996).**

Open Meetings A.G. Opinions After 1988

A public body holding an open meeting in compliance with the Open Meetings Act may recess the open meeting to hold subquorum committee meetings for which no public notice has been posted, provided no quorum of the public body will be present at the committee meetings, the committees are purely advisory in nature, and deliberation on a common topic leading to a decision by the public body does not take place among the committees. **Op. Atty. Gen. 1994, No. 6752.**

The meetings of site review boards remain subject to the Open Meetings Act, despite the Type II transfer, a transfer of an existing department or agency to a principal department, of these boards by Executive Order 1991-31. **Op. Atty. Gen. 1994, No. 6799.**

Conviction of a city council member for violating the Open Meetings Act does not result in a vacancy in office under state law. **Op. Atty. Gen. 1994, No. 6800.**

Sections 7 and 8 of the Open Meetings Act, which authorize closed sessions for deliberations on certain enumerated topics, apply only to deliberations, not decisions. **Op. Atty. Gen. 1994, No. 6817.**

Public bodies must take minutes of a closed session that reflect the date, time, place, members present and absent, and the purpose or purposes of the closed session. **Op. Atty. Gen. 1994, No. 6817.**

While the Open Meetings Act does not require that notice of a special meeting state the specific nature of all action to be taken at the meeting, MCL 41.72a [a statute applicable to such townships] does require a general law township board to state in its notice the business to be transacted at the meeting. **Op. Atty. Gen. 1994, No. 6821.**

An intermediate school district may permit some representatives of constituent district boards to attend its annual budget meeting by means of interactive television. **Op. Atty. Gen. 1995, No. 6835.**

Appendix 11

FREEDOM OF INFORMATION ACT ATTORNEY GENERAL'S OPINIONS

(For update see http://www.ag.state.mi.us/)

1. Unless exempt from disclosure by law, records of the Brown-McNeeley insurance fund are public records. **Attorney General Opinion No. 5156, p. 66, March 24, 1977.**

2. The FOIA's definition of public body includes single member bodies. **Attorney General Opinion No. 5183-A, p. 97, April 18, 1977.**

3. Records subject to the confidentiality provisions of the Child Protection Law, **MCL 722.621 et seq; MSA 25.248(1) et seq**, are exempt from disclosure under the FOIA, §§ 13(1)(a) and 13(1)(d). **Attorney General Opinion No. 5297, p. 430, April 28, 1978.**

4. The office of county sheriff is subject to the provisions of the Freedom of Information Act. **Attorney General Opinion No. 5419, p. 758, December 29, 1978.**

5. Since certain records are protected from disclosure by the Social Welfare Act, they are exempt from disclosure under section 13(1)(d) of the Freedom of Information Act which exempts records that are exempt from disclosure by statute. **Attorney General Opinion No. 5436, p. 31, February 1, 1979.**

6. The Insurance Commissioner is required to charge a rate for making copies of public records requested in accordance with the Freedom of Information Act. **Attorney General Opinion No. 5465, p. 104, March 26, 1979.**

7. The following responses to specific inquiries are found in **Attorney General Opinion No. 5500, published on July 23, 1979.**

a. A summary of the Freedom of Information Act. p. 255

b. A government agency does not fall within the meaning of "person" for purposes of obtaining information under the Act. p. 261

c. The Civil Service Commission is subject to the provisions of the Freedom of Information Act. p. 261

d. Since the President's Council of State Colleges and Universities is wholly funded by state universities and colleges, it is a public body as defined by the Freedom of Information Act. p. 262

e. A board of trustees of a county hospital may refuse to make available records of its proceedings or reports received and records compiled which would constitute a clearly unwarranted invasion of an individual's privacy under section 13(1)(a), involve disclosure of medical, counseling or psychological facts or evaluations concerning a named individual under section 13(m); or involve disclosure that would violate physician-patient or psychologist-patient privilege under section 13(1)(i). p. 263

f. Transcripts of depositions taken in the course of an administrative hearing are subject to disclosure to a person who was not a party to the proceeding, as there is no specific exemption in section 13(1) or any other statute which exempts a deposition or a document referring to the deposition from disclosure. These documents may, however, contain statements which are exempt from disclosure and therefore, pursuant to section 14, where a person who is not a party to the proceeding requests a copy, it will be necessary to separate the exempt material and make only the nonexempt records available. p. 263

g. Stenographer's notes or the tape recordings or dictaphone records of a municipal meeting used to prepare minutes are public records under the Act and must be made available to the public. p. 264

h. Computer software developed by and in the possession of a public body is not a public record. p. 264

i. Although a state university must release a report of the performance of its official functions in its files, regardless of who prepared it, if a report prepared by an outside agency is retained only by the private agency, it is not subject to public disclosure. p. 265

j. Copyrighted materials are not subject to the Act. p. 266

k. A request for data which refers only to an extensive period of time and contains no other reference by which the public record may be found does not comply with the requirement of section 3 that the request describe the public record sufficiently to enable the public body to find it. p. 268

l. If a public body maintains a file of the names of employees which it has fired or suspended over a certain designated period of time, it must disclose the list if requested. p. 268

m. A public body may charge a fee for providing a copy of a public record. p. 268

n. The five-day response provision begins the day after the public body has received the request sufficiently describing the public record. If the request does not contain sufficient information describing the public record, it may be denied on that ground. Subsequently, if additional information is provided that sufficiently describes the public record, the period within which the response must be made dates from the time that the additional information is received. p. 269

o. A school board may meet in closed session pursuant to the Open Meetings Act to consider matters which are exempt from disclosure under the Freedom of Information Act. p. 270

p. The names and addresses of students may be released unless the parent of the student or the student has informed the institution in writing that such information should not be released. p. 282

q. A law enforcement agency may refuse to release the name of a person who has been arrested, but not charged, in a complaint or information, with the commission of a crime. p. 282

r. Since motor vehicle registration lists have not been declared to be confidential, they are required to be open to public inspection. p. 300

8. File photographs routinely taken of criminal suspects by law enforcement agencies are public records as defined by the Freedom of Information Act. To the extent that the release of a photograph of a person would constitute a clearly unwarranted invasion of personal privacy, a public body may refuse to permit a person to inspect or make copies of the photograph. **Attorney General Opinion No. 5593, p. 468, November 14, 1979.**

9. The exemption contained in section 13(1)(n) of the Freedom of Information Act for communications and notes within a public body or between public bodies of an advisory nature does not constitute an exemption for the purposes of the Open Meetings Act in view of a specific statutory provision which states that this exemption does not constitute an exemption for the purposes of section 8(h) of the Open Meetings Act. **Attorney General Opinion No. 5608, p. 496, December 17, 1979.**

10. The meetings of a board of education expelling a student from school must list a student's name. Unedited minutes must be furnished to the public on request in accordance with law. **Attorney General Opinion No. 5632, p. 563, January 24, 1980.**

11. The confidentiality mandated by the Banking Code of 1969 is not limited to facts and information furnished by state chartered banks, but applies to all facts and information received by the Financial Institutions Bureau. Such facts and information are not subject to disclosure

pursuant to the Freedom of Information Act. **Attorney General Opinion No. 5725, p. 842, June 23, 1980**.

12. Rules promulgated by the Ethics Board require that records and files concerning dismissed complaints or terminated investigations be suppressed or expunged. This rule is consistent with the privacy exemption of the FOIA since records would be suppressed only if a determination was made that the complaints were unfounded. **Attorney General Opinion No. 5760, p 935, August 26, 1980**.

13. Since the Law Enforcement Information Network Policy Council does not receive and maintain records in the LIEN system, it does not possess copies of records and as a result has no material to furnish persons seeking such records under the Freedom of Information Act. **Attorney General Opinion No. 5797, p. 1038, October 14, 1980**.

14. A public body is not required to disclose both the questions and answers of a sheriff's promotional test unless the public body finds it in the public interest to disclose both the test questions and answers. **Attorney General Opinion No. 5832, p. 1125, December 18, 1980**.

15. Employment records disclosing salary history and employment dates are subject to disclosure under the Freedom of Information Act. **Attorney General Opinion No. 6019, p. 507, December 29, 1981**.

16. Copies of receipts maintained by a register of deeds for amounts paid as real estate transfer taxes fall within the mandatory exemption from disclosure established by 1966 P.A. 134, section 11b, and are exempt from disclosure under the Freedom of Information Act. **Attorney General Opinion No. 6023, p. 518, January 8, 1982**.

17. A township is not required to enact its own Freedom of Information Act in order to comply with the state Freedom of Information Act. **Attorney General Opinion No. 6042, p. 584, February 25, 1982**.

18. A school district must furnish the records of a student upon request of another school district in which the student is enrolled as an incident to the operation of free public elementary and secondary schools required by the Michigan Constitution 1963, art. 8, section 2, and is precluded from withholding the records because the student or his or her parents is indebted to the school district possessing the records for fees or other charges. **Attorney General Opinion No. 6064, p. 641, April 30, 1982**.

19. Records of a public body showing the number of days a public employee is absent from work are not exempt from disclosure under the Freedom of Information Act. **Attorney General Opinion No. 6087, p. 698, July 28, 1982**.

20. The Freedom of Information Act does not require a sheriff to furnish jail booking records to a private security firm if the sheriff determines disclosure would constitute a clearly unwarranted invasion of privacy. **Attorney General Opinion No. 6389, p. 374, September 24, 1986**.

21. State legislators are exempt from the Freedom of Information Act. **Attorney General Opinion No. 6390, p. 375, September 26, 1986**.

22. Surveys, comments, and other information received by the Qualifications Advisory Committee in its performance evaluation of worker's compensation magistrates are confidential by statute, MCL 418.212(1)(g), and, therefore, are exempt from disclosure under the FOIA. **Attorney General Opinion No. 6504, p. 295, March 4, 1988**.

23. The FOIA does not apply to a private nonprofit corporation. **Attorney General Opinion No. 6563, p. 27, January 26, 1989**.

24. While the personal files of the Auditor General are exempt from disclosure, the general files, records, and final audit reports prepared by the Auditor General's staff are subject to FOIA disclosure, except where a portion is specifically exempted by statute. **Attorney General Opinion No. 6613, p. 299, March 14, 1990**.

25. A public officer's or employee's routine performance evaluation is not exempt from disclosure, even when the evaluation is discussed in a closed meeting held pursuant to the Open Meetings Act. **Attorney General Opinion No. 6668, p. 409, November 28, 1990**.

26. A public body may not deny a FOIA request simply because the requester has previously obtained the identical records under that statute. A public body need not provide a waiver of fees to an indigent person requesting additional copies of identical documents previously provided with a waiver of fees pursuant to a prior request under the FOIA. **Attorney General Opinion No. 6766, p. 52, August 19, 1993**.

27. The records maintained by the Department of State Police on the STATIS computer system meet the definition of a "public record" set forth in section 2(c) of the FOIA. Therefore, that Department must search the STATIS computer system when it responds to a FOIA request. It must also allow the examination of or produce copies of all documents it finds, unless the records sought fall within one or more of the specific exemptions set forth in section 13 of the FOIA. Although participating law enforcement agencies other than the Department of State Police have remote computer terminals, which allow them access to the STATIS computer, those records are not writings in the possession of those agencies within the meaning of the FOIA, section 2(c) and (e), unless those records are saved to a computer storage device or printed by the participating agency. Thus, law enforcement agencies other than the Department of State Police are not obligated under the FOIA to search the STATIS system for records except for those

records which they contributed to that system. **Attorney General Opinion No. 6820, p. 196, October 11, 1994**.

28. Section 4(2) of the Freedom of Information Act permits a public body to charge a deposit of not more than one-half of the projected total fee if that fee exceeds $50.00. A public body may establish a fee in advance of compiling the records responsive to a request under the Freedom of Information Act so long as the fee represents the actual cost of responding to the request based on prior experience and it is calculated in accordance with section 4 of the Freedom of Information Act. **Attorney General Opinion No. 6923, p 224, October 23, 1996**.

29. A private, voluntary unincorporated association of lake property owners is not a public body subject to the FOIA. A corporation formed under the summer resort owners corporation act, 1929 PA 137, **MCL 455.201 et seq., MSA 21.751 et seq.**, is a public body subject to the provisions of the FOIA. **Attorney General Opinion No. 6942, p 40, July 3, 1997**.

30. The state Insurance Bureau, in response to a request made under the Freedom of Information Act, 1976 PA 442, must provide copies of copyrighted manuals of rules and rates which are in its possession and are required by law to be filed by insurers with the bureau, without first obtaining the permission of the copyright holder. **Attorney General Opinion No. 6965, p 91, January 16, 1998**.

31. Under the FOIA, the Auditor General may, in the discharge of his duties to audit the states and its departments, access non-exempt public records of local units of government under the Freedom of Information Act. **Attorney General Opinion No. 6970, p 106, January 28, 1998**.

32. A public body may require that its fees be paid in full prior to actual delivery of the copies. However, a public body may not refuse to process a subsequent FOIA request on the ground that the requestor failed to pay fees charged for a prior FOIA request. A public body may refuse to process a FOIA request if the requestor fails to pay a good faith deposit properly requested by the public body pursuant to section 4(2) of the FOIA.

Although the FOIA does not specify a limitations period within which a public body must commence a lawsuit to collect fees charged for complying with a records request, the 6-year limitations period applicable to contract claims governs such a cause of action. **Attorney General Opinion No. 6977, p , April 1, 1998**.

Court Opinions on the Freedom of Information Act

<u>Herald Co.</u> v <u>Bay City</u>, 228 Mich App 268; 577 NW2d 696 (1998).

Information about a person being considered as a finalist for a high level public position is not of a "personal nature" for the purposes of the FOIA privacy exemption. Once the list of candidates has been narrowed to those persons to be interviewed, the applicant's right of privacy is outweighed by the public's interest in knowing the applicants' qualifications. Redaction can be used to separate confidential information from non-private information.

<u>Bradley</u> v <u>Saranac Community Schools Board of Education</u>, 455 Mich 285; 565 NW2d 650 (1997).

The Michigan FOIA does not have a specific exemption for personnel records. Thus, the personnel records of non-law enforcement public employees generally are available to the public. Information that falls within one of the exemptions of the FOIA may be redacted.

The privacy exemption under 13(1)(a) of the FOIA consists of two elements, both of which must be met in order for an exemption to apply. First, the information must be of a "personal nature." Second, the disclosure must be a "clearly unwarranted invasion of privacy."

Performance appraisals, disciplinary actions, and complaints relating to employees' accomplishments in their public jobs do not reveal intimate or embarrassing details of their private lives and, therefore, they are not records of a "personal nature."

Performance evaluations of public employees are not counseling evaluations protected from disclosure by the FOIA, §13(1)(m).

Section 13(1)(n) of the FOIA provides an exemption for communications passing within or between public bodies. Documents in the possession of a school district prepared by parents are not within the scope of this exemption. Further, the exemption must be asserted by a public body rather than by a private individual.

<u>Seaton</u> v <u>Wayne County Prosecutor</u>, 225 Mich App 1; 570 NW2d 125 (1997).

A prisoner's request for records pertaining to his own criminal conviction is governed exclusively by court rule, MCR 6.101(L), now MCR 6.433(A). The FOIA does not apply.

<u>Herald Co.</u> v <u>Ann Arbor Public Schools</u>, 224 Mich App 266; 568 NW2d 411 (1997).

Once a document that is the subject of a FOIA lawsuit has been disclosed, the subject of the controversy disappears and becomes moot.

The privacy exemption of the FOIA allows a public body to withhold from disclosure public records of a personal nature where the information would constitute a clearly unwarranted invasion of an individual's privacy. Information is considered personal if it concerns a particular person and his intimate affairs, interests or activities. While the records sought in this case were personal in nature in that they contained information about a teacher's family and observations about his conduct, the disclosure did not constitute a "clearly unwarranted" invasion of privacy because the records discussed the professional performance of a teacher in the classroom which is an issue of legitimate concern to the public.

A public body may exempt from disclosure, pursuant to section 13(1)(n), advisory communications within a public body or between public bodies to the extent that they are non-factual and are preliminary to a final agency determination. However, if records meet these substantive tests, the public body must also establish that the public interest in encouraging frank communications within the public body or between public bodies clearly outweighs the public interest in disclosure. In this case the public interest in disclosing records that contain public observations of a teacher who has been convicted of carrying a concealed weapon is not clearly outweighed by the public interest in encouraging frank communications within the public body. A class of documents may be exempt from the FOIA so long as the exempt categories are clearly described and drawn with precision so that all documents within a category are similar in nature. Exempt material must be segregated from non-exempt material to the extent practicable.

The FOIA exempts, in section 13(1)(i), information subject to the physician-patient privilege. The purpose of the privilege is to protect the physician-patient relationship and ensure that communications between the two are confidential. Attendance records that do not contain any information that a physician acquired while treating an employee are not covered by this exemption.

The fact that an employee waives the physician-patient privilege by submitting to his employer attendance records that contain medical records does not mean that the privilege was waived with regard to third parties who request disclosure of the records under the FOIA.

The FOIA excludes from disclosure information protected by the attorney-client privilege. The scope of the privilege is narrow, including only those communications by the client to its advisor that are made for the purpose of obtaining legal advice. A tape recording of an interview of the teacher by the school district is not within the attorney-client privilege.

CMU Supervisory- Technical Ass'n MEA/NEA v CMU Board of Trustees, 223 Mich App 727; 567 NW2d 696 (1997).

A party to a lawsuit does not lose his right under the FOIA simply because the party may be able to obtain the records from a public body through the discovery phase of pending civil litigation.

Oakland County Prosecutor v Department of Corrections, 222 Mich App 654; 564 NW2d 922 (1997).

A prisoner's mental health records submitted to the parole board when seeking parole must be provided to a county prosecutor when requested pursuant to FOIA so that the prosecutor may determine whether the board's decision to grant parole should be appealed.

The records are not exempt from disclosure under the psychologist-patient privilege because the prisoner in seeking parole consents to the release of the records to the parole board. Once otherwise privileged records are disclosed to a third party by the holder of the privilege, the privilege disappears.

The records are not exempt pursuant to a statutory provision protecting records created in the course of providing mental health services because that provision permits release to "comply with another provision of law" i.e. a prosecutor's request for such records to determine whether to appeal a particular parole.

Section 13(1)(m) of the FOIA which exempts psychological evaluations concerning an individual if the disclosure would reveal the identity of the individual is inapplicable because the identity of the individual is already known.

The privacy exemption at section 13(1)(a) of the FOIA is not applicable. Notwithstanding the personal nature of the records sought, the invasion is warranted because the Legislature has provided for the release of these records in the context of the parole proceedings.

Schroeder v Detroit, 221 Mich App 364; 561 NW2d 497 (1997).

A person denied employment by a police department was not entitled to receive a copy of his psychological evaluation under the FOIA. In cases involving testing instruments as defined by section 13(1)(l) of the FOIA, release of the information is not required unless the public interest in disclosure outweighs the public interest in non-disclosure. Here, the public interest ensuring the integrity of the hiring process outweighed the public interest in disclosing the information to a candidate attempting to investigate the fairness of the test.

Grebner v Oakland County Clerk, 220 Mich App 513; 560 NW2d 351 (1996).

Section 10(1) of the FOIA is a combined jurisdiction and venue provision. This provision makes it clear that circuit courts have jurisdiction to hear FOIA cases and specifies the counties in which the action may be brought.

Venue for FOIA actions properly lies in the county where the complainant resides.

Nicita v Detroit, 216 Mich App 746; 550 NW2d 269 (1996).

Business records pertaining to a real estate development company are not exempt from disclosure pursuant to § 13(1)(a) of the FOIA where there is no indication that the records contain information of a personal nature. This section does not protect information that could conceivably lead to the revelation of personal information.

Section 13(1)(n) of the FOIA protects communications within or between a public body that are other than purely factual and are preliminary to a final agency determination of policy or action. A public agency must also show that the need for non-disclosure clearly outweighs the public interest in disclosure.

Grebner v Clinton Charter Twp, 216 Mich App 736; 440 NW2d 265 (1996).

Section 522(1) of the Michigan Election Law which provides for the making, certifying, and delivery of a computer tape to any person upon the payment to the clerk of the court of the cost of making, certifying and delivering the tape, disk, or listing is not a statute "specifically authorizing the sale" of the computer tape. Therefore, the determination of the fee to be charged for obtaining the computer tape is made pursuant to § 4 of the FOIA.

Lansing Ass'n of School Adm'rs v Lansing School District, 216 Mich App 79; 549 NW2d 15 (1996).

Plaintiffs seeking to prevent a school board from disclosing personnel records of employees must predicate their suits on grounds outside of the FOIA. No abuse of discretion was found in the school board's decision to release documents where the release of the information did not infringe on the common law or constitutional privacy rights of the plaintiffs.

Eric Jackson v Eastern Michigan University, 215 Mich App 240; 544 NW2d 737 (1996).

Eastern Michigan University Foundation is primarily funded by Eastern Michigan University and, therefore, is a public body subject to FOIA.

Michigan Council of Trout Unlimited v Michigan Department of Military Affairs, 213 Mich App 203; 539 NW2d 745 (1995).

Notwithstanding the unique relationship between the Michigan National Guard and the Federal Government which is explicitly recognized by Michigan statutes, the circuit court had jurisdiction to consider plaintiff's actions under the Michigan FOIA seeking to obtain documents in possession of the Michigan National Guard.

While the state courts have jurisdiction, application of § 13(1)(d) of the Michigan FOIA encompasses federal regulations and the federal FOIA both of which prohibit the release of the documents sought by plaintiff. Accordingly, plaintiff could not obtain the documents at issue.

Thomas v State Board of Law Examiners, 210 Mich App 279; 533 NW2d 3 (1995).

The State Board of Law Examiner's is an agent of the judiciary and, therefore, not a public body subject to the disclosure requirements of the FOIA.

Farrell v Detroit, 209 Mich App 7; 530 NW2d 105 (1995).

Computer records are public records that are subject to disclosure pursuant to the FOIA. A public body is required to provide public records in the form requested, not just the information they contain. The providing of a computer printout of the information contained on a computer tape does not satisfy a request for the computer tape itself.

Local 312 of the AFSCME, AFL-CIO v Detroit, 207 Mich App 472; 525 NW2d 487 (1994).

The public employment relations act (PERA) and the freedom of information act (FOIA) are not conflicting statutes such that the PERA would prevail over the FOIA with the result that a person involved in a labor dispute would be precluded from obtaining public records under the FOIA. The Legislature has clearly defined the class of persons entitled to seek disclosure of public records pursuant to the FOIA. There is no sound policy reason for distinguishing between persons who are involved in litigation-type proceedings and those who are not. The court is required to award plaintiff attorney fees and costs where the plaintiff prevails in a FOIA action.

In Re Subpoena Duces Tecum, on remand from the MI Supreme Court, 205 Mich App 700; 518 NW2d 522 (1994).

Section 13(1)(n) of the FOIA protects from disclosure communications within or between public bodies of an advisory nature that are other than purely factual and are preliminary to a final agency determination of policy or action. The burden is on the public body to show, in each particular instance, that the public interest in encouraging frank communications between officials and employees of the public body clearly outweighs the public interest in disclosure. It is not adequate to show that the requested document falls within a general category of documents that may be protected.

Hyson v Department of Corrections, 205 Mich App 422; 521 NW2d 841 (1994).

Statements made by confidential witnesses relating to a major misconduct charge against a prison inmate may be withheld when requested pursuant to FOIA because disclosure of the documents, even with the names of the witnesses deleted, would reveal their identities and jeopardize their personal safety within the prison. In addition, the release would prejudice the public body's ability to maintain the physical security of the penal institution.

Mackey v Department of Corrections, 205 Mich App 330; 517 NW2d 303 (1994).

A prison record about a prison inmate is exempt from disclosure under the prison security exemption of the FOIA where the record is requested by an inmate other than the one to whom the record pertains.

The Detroit News, Inc v Detroit, 204 Mich App 720; 516 NW2d 151 (1994).

Telephone bills paid by a public body constitute expense records of public officials and employees and are "public records" under the FOIA.

Quatrine v Mackinaw City Public Schools, 204 Mich App 342; 514 NW2d 254 (1994).

Public schools were not required to release records under FOIA where written parental consent for release of records was not provided.

Newark Morning Ledger Company v Saginaw County Sheriff, 204 Mich App 215; 514 NW2d 213 (1994).

Internal affairs investigation records of a law enforcement agency constitute personnel records which are exempt from disclosure, unless the public interest in disclosure outweighs the public interest in non-disclosure. The mere location of a public record in a personnel file is not determinative as to its status in a personnel record.

In determining what is a "personnel record" under the FOIA the court looked to the definition of that term in the Bullard-Plawecki Employee Right to Know Act (ERKA). While the purpose of the FOIA and the ERKA are different, the Legislature's clearly expressed intent in the ERKA to prohibit access by an employee to any internal investigations relating to that employee indicates an intent to not allow public access to such records.

Densmore v Department of Corrections, 203 Mich App 363; 512 NW2d 72 (1994).

A public body does not need to provide additional copies of records it has already provided unless the requester can demonstrate why the copy already provided was not sufficient.

Booth Newspapers, Inc v University of Michigan Board of Regents, 444 Mich 211; 507 NW2d 422 (1993).

To exempt information under the FOIA, § 13(1)(a), information must be of "personal nature," and disclosure of that information must constitute "clearly unwarranted" invasion of privacy. Travel expense records of members of a public body do not constitute "records of a personal nature."

The privacy exemption does not permit the withholding of information that conceivably could lead to the revelation of personal information. Therefore, a public body may not withhold travel expense records because their disclosure might lead to information concerning the candidates interviewed by board members.

Walen v Department of Corrections, 443 Mich 240; 505 NW2d 519 (1993).

A prison disciplinary hearing falls within the definition of "contested case" and, therefore, pursuant to the FOIA, § 11(1), must be published and made available to the public. The Department of Corrections satisfied the publication requirement by retaining the final orders and decisions from disciplinary hearings in prisoners' files.

Patterson v Allegan County Sheriff, 199 Mich App 638; 502 NW2d 368 (1993)

A booking photograph of a county jail inmate kept in the files of a county sheriff is a public record under the FOIA; such photographs may not be withheld from disclosure on the basis of the privacy exemption found in 13 (1) (a).

Yarbrough v Department of Corrections, 199 Mich App 180; 501 NW2d 207 (1993)

Records compiled in the course of an internal investigation into a sexual harassment are "investigating records compiled for law enforcement purposes" within the meaning of said terms at § 13(1)(b) of the FOIA.

Hubka v Pennfield Township, 197 Mich App 117, 494 NW2d 800 (1992)

Letters sent by a township attorney to a township board that contain information obtained by the attorney from township employees under compulsion and promises of confidentiality are protected from disclosure under the Freedom of Information Act by the attorney-client privilege. Likewise, the opinions, conclusions, and recommendations of the attorney, based on the information, are protected.

Wilson v Eaton Rapids, 196 Mich App 671; 493 NW2d 433 (1992)

A public body's attempt to reconcile a contractual obligation to maintain the confidentiality of a resignation agreement with its statutory obligation under FOIA does not constitute arbitrary and capricious behavior.

A party prevails under FOIA, and is therefore entitled to an award of costs and reasonable attorney fees, only if the action was necessary to and had a substantial causative effect on delivery or access to the documents.

Swickard v Wayne County Medical Examiner, 196 Mich App 98; 492 NW2d 497 (1992)

A party who prevails completely in an action asserting the right to inspect or receive a copy of a public record under the Freedom of Information Act is entitled to reasonable attorney fees, costs, and disbursements. No time limit is imposed upon a prevailing party for requesting attorney fees.

Nicita v Detroit, 194 Mich App 657; 487 NW2d 814 (1992)

Section 13 (l) (j) of the FOIA does not exempt bids with respect to development projects from disclosure once a developer has been chosen.

Shellum v MESC, 194 Mich App 474; 487 NW2d 490 (1992)

Information held by MESC concerning the calculated unemployment insurance tax contribution rate of an employer is exempt from disclosure under 13 (1) (d) of the FOIA because it utilizes information obtained from the employer which is protected by statute and administrative rule.

Swickard v Wayne County Medical Examiner, 438 Mich 536; 475 NW2d 304 (1991)

In making a determination whether a disclosure of requested information would constitute an invasion of privacy one looks to constitutional law and common law as well as customs, mores, or ordinary views of the community.

The release of autopsy reports and toxicology test results are not unwarranted infringements on the right to privacy of either the deceased or the deceased's family. The autopsy report and toxicology tests are not within the doctor-patient privilege.

Michigan Tax Management Services Co v City of Warren, 437 Mich 506; 473 NW2d 263 (1991)

When a prevailing party in a FOIA action is awarded "reasonable" attorney fees, the trial court is obligated to make an independent determination with regard to the amount of the fee. The standard utilized by an appellate court to review such a determination is abuse of discretion.

Favors v Department of Corrections, 192 Mich App 131; 480 NW2d 604 (1991)

The form used in determining whether a prisoner should be awarded disciplinary credits was exempt from disclosure under §13(1)(n) of the FOIA in that it covered other than purely factual materials, was advisory in nature and preliminary to final agency determination of policy or action.

The public interest in encouraging frank communications within the Department of Corrections (DOC) clearly outweighed the public interest in disclosure of worksheet forms. The trial court failed to comply with the technical requirements of FOIA because it did not require the DOC to bear the burden of proving that a public record was exempt. However, that failure did not require reversal of a grant of summary disposition for the DOC in inmate's action where the DOC clearly reached the correct result.

Lepp v Cheboygan Area Schools, 190 Mich App 726; 476 NW2d 506 (1991)

Where the requested information pertains to the party making the request, it is unreasonable to refuse disclosure on the grounds of invasion of privacy.

Clerical-Technical Union of MSU v Board of Trustees of MSU, 190 Mich App 300; 475 NW2d 373 (1991).

The home addresses of donors to Michigan State University are information of a personal nature, the disclosure of which would constitute a clearly unwarranted invasion of privacy.

The Detroit News, Inc v Detroit, 185 Mich App 296; 460 NW2d 312 (1990)

The minutes of a closed city council meeting, held in violation of Open meetings Act, are public records and are available upon request under the FOIA.

The oral opinions of an attorney are not public records subject to the FOIA and, therefore, cannot be used to justify a closed meeting of a public body.

Wayne County Prosecutor v Detroit, 185 Mich App 265; 460 NW2d 298 (1990)

For purposes of the FOIA, a county prosecutor is a person as defined in the Act. This allows him, in his official capacity, to request documents from public bodies under the FOIA.

Traverse City Record Eagle v Traverse City Area Public Schools, 184 Mich App 609; 459 NW2d 28 (1990)

A tentative bargaining agreement between a school district and the union which represents its employees was held to be exempt from disclosure pursuant to § 13(1)(n) of the FOIA which exempts communication and notes within a public body or between public bodies which are advisory, nonfactual and preliminary to a final decision. The public interest in encouraging frank communications between the employer and its employees, which leads to effective negotiations, in this case outweighs the public interest in disclosure.

Hartzell v Mayville Community School District, 183 Mich App 782; 455 NW2d 411 (1990)

The FOIA requires disclosure of the fact that a requested document does not exist. A plaintiff in a FOIA action that is forced to file a lawsuit to ascertain that a document does not exist is a prevailing party entitled to an award of costs and reasonable attorney fees.

Tallman v Cheboygan Area Schools, 183 Mich App 123; 454 NW2d 171 (1990)

A public body may charge a fee for providing a copy of a public record. Section 4 of the Act provides a method for determining the charge for records and a public body is obligated to arrive at its fees pursuant to that section.

Booth Newspapers, Inc v Kalamazoo School District, 181 Mich App 752; 450 NW2d 286 (1989)

The trial court appropriately ordered the release of tenure charges and a settlement agreement concerning allegations of sexual misconduct against an unmarried teacher in redacted form. The records were redacted to prevent the identity of the teacher and the students involved from being disclosed in order to protect their privacy.

The FOIA confers discretion upon a court to award an appropriate portion of the reasonable attorney fees incurred by a party which has prevailed in part. When a plaintiff prevails only as to a portion of the request, the award of fees should be fairly allocable to that portion.

Kincaid v Department of Corrections, 180 Mich App 176; 446 NW2d 604 (1989)

A public body bears the burden of proof in demonstrating a proper justification for the denial of a FOIA request.

A request for disclosure of information under the FOIA must describe the requested records sufficiently to enable the public body to find them; when a request is denied because of an insufficient description, the requesting person may (1) rewrite the request with additional information, or (2) file suit in circuit court where the sole issue would be the sufficiency of information to describe the records desired.

A FOIA request by an inmate which erroneously states the date of a guilty determination on a misconduct or the hearing date with respect to which records are sought, reasonably and sufficiently describes the records sought. A public body acts in an arbitrary and capricious manner by repeatedly refusing to look for a record so described.

Post-Newsweek Stations, Michigan, Inc v Detroit, 179 Mich App 331; 445 NW2d 529 (1989)

In claiming an exemption under FOIA, for interference with law enforcement proceedings, the burden of proof is on the public body claiming the exemption. The exemption must be interpreted narrowly and the public body must separate exempt material from non-exempt and make non-exempt information available. Exempt information must be described with particularity indicating how the information would interfere with law enforcement proceedings.

When analyzing claims of exemption under FOIA a trial court must make sure it receives a complete particularized justification for a denial of a request, or hold in camera hearings to determine whether this justification exists. The court may allow counsel for the requesting party to examine, in camera, under special agreement, the contested material.

<u>Easley</u> v <u>University of Michigan</u>, 178 Mich App 723; 444 NW2d 820 (1989)

A public body must have in its possession or control a copy of the requested document before it can be produced or before a court can order its production.

<u>Payne</u> v <u>Grand Rapids Police Chief</u>, 178 Mich App 193; 443 NW2d 481 (1989)

A record of a law enforcement investigation may be exempt from disclosure under the FOIA where disclosure would interfere with law enforcement proceedings. However, the agency must demonstrate how disclosure of particular records or kinds of records would amount to interference on the basis of facts and not merely conclusory statements which recite the language of the act.

A court can consider allowing plaintiff's counsel to have access to contested records in camera under special agreement as a means to resolve a FOIA lawsuit.

<u>Booth Newspapers, Inc</u> v <u>Kent County Treasurer</u>, 175 Mich App 523; 438 NW2d 317 (1989)

Tax records indicating the monthly or quarterly tax payments made by individual hotels and motels under a county hotel/motel tax do not fall within the FOIA's privacy exemption.

<u>Hagen</u> v <u>Department of Education</u>, 431 Mich 118; 427 NW2d 879 (1988)

The decisions of the State Tenure Commission are matters of public record. When a private hearing is requested by a teacher as provided under the teacher tenure act, the decision may be withheld during the administrative stage of the teacher's appeal. Once a final administrative decision is reached, the decision may not be withheld from disclosure.

<u>Oakland Press</u> v <u>Pontiac Stadium Building Authority</u>, 173 Mich App 41; 433 NW2d 317 (1988)

The release of names and addresses of licensees doing business with a public body is not an unwarranted invasion of privacy.

Haskins v **Oronoko Township Supervisor**, 172 Mich App 73; 431 NW2d 210 (1988)

A trial court complies with the holding in **The Evening News Ass'n** v **City of Troy**, 417 Mich 481; 339 NW2d 421 (1983), where it conducts an in camera inspection of the records sought and determines that certain records are exempt from disclosure under narrowly drawn statutory exemptions designed to protect the identity of confidential informants.

Kubick v **Child and Family Services of Michigan**, 171 Mich App 304; 429 NW2d 881 (1988)

While there is no bright-line rule to determine what constitutes "primarily funded" to determine if a body is a "public body" as defined at §2(b) of the act, a private nonprofit corporation which receives less than half of its funding from government sources is not a public body which is primarily funded by or through state or local authority. Accordingly, such corporation is not subject to the requirements of the Freedom of Information Act regarding the disclosure of information by public bodies.

Kearney v **Department of Mental Health**, 168 Mich App 406; 425 NW2d 161 (1988)

The FOIA exempts from disclosure records exempted from disclosure by other statutory authority. Mental Health treatment records are exempt under the Mental Health Code. However, treatment records may be disclosed where the holder of the record and the patient consent.

Persons requesting records under the FOIA are not entitled to free copies of the records. The holder of a public record may charge a fee for providing copies. There is, however, a waiver of the first $20.00 for those who, by affidavit, can show an inability to pay because of indigency.

State Employees Association v **Department of Management & Budget**, 428 Mich 104; 404 NW2d 606 (1987)

The disclosure of the home addresses of state employees to a recognized employee organization does not constitute a clearly unwarranted invasion of privacy.

Residential Ratepayer Consortium v **Public Service Commission**, 168 Mich App 476; 425 NW2d 98 (1987)

An administrative agency does not waive its defenses in a circuit court action to compel disclosure of documents under FOIA because they were not raised at the administrative level.

Jones v **Wayne County Prosecutor's Office**, 165 Mich App 62; 418 NW2d 667 (1987)

A criminal defendant seeking documents pertaining to his criminal conviction must seek those records from the court pursuant to court rule, not from the prosecutor pursuant to FOIA.

Detroit Free Press, Inc v Oakland County Sheriff, 164 Mich App 656; 418 NW2d 124 (1987)

Booking photographs of persons arrested, charged with felonies, and awaiting trial are not protected from release as an unwarranted invasion of personal privacy.

Mithrandir v Department of Corrections, 164 Mich App 143; 416 NW2d 352 (1987)

Because of the special circumstances surrounding prison security and the confinement of prisoners, the Department of Corrections may set limits on a prisoner's right to examine nonexempt records.

Walloon Lake Water System, Inc v Melrose Township, 163 Mich App 726; 415 NW2d 292 (1987)

A public body does not escape liability under the FOIA merely because a capricious act on its part rendered the lawsuit moot. This is particularly true when actions of the public body include direct violation of the FOIA, i.e., not giving a written explanation of the refusal as required and willfully disposing of the material knowing that a suit is pending under the FOIA for disclosure.

Laracey v Financial Institutions Bureau, 163 Mich App 437; 414 NW2d 909 (1987)

Attorney who filed pro se action is not entitled to recover attorney fees in a FOIA lawsuit.

DeMaria Building Co, Inc v Department of Management and Budget, 159 Mich App 729; 407 NW2d 72 (1987)

The exemption found in 13 (1) (n) of the FOIA, for communications and notes within a public body or between public bodies, does not apply to an outside consultant's report to a public body.
In re Buchanan, 152 Mich App 706; 394 NW2d 78 (1986)

The common-law right of access to court records is not without limitation.

Health Central v Commissioner of Insurance, 152 Mich App 336; 393 NW2d 625 (1986)

HMO's have no standing to raise common-law right of privacy claims. Such claims can only be asserted by individuals whose privacy has been invaded. The right of privacy does not protect artificial entities.

Curry v Jackson Circuit Court, 151 Mich App 754; 391 NW2d 476 (1986)

The term "resides" as used in the FOIA, when applied to a prisoner, refers to the prisoner's intended domicile. Such a place may be the county where the prisoner last lived before being sent to prison or the county where the prison is located. Factors such as the possibility of parole and how the prisoner has ordered his personal business transactions will be considered relevant to corroboration of a prisoner's stated intention relative to domicile.

Milford v Gilb, 148 Mich App 778; 384 NW2d 786 (1985)

Under the FOIA a public body may exempt from disclosure communications and notes within a public body or between public bodies of an advisory nature to the extent that they cover other than purely factual materials. The public body bears the burden of proof that a statutory exception applies to the item requested.

Paprocki v Jackson County Clerk, 142 Mich App 785; 371 NW2d 450 (1985)

Under 10(1) of FOIA, the term "resides," when applied to a prisoner, refers to the place where the prisoner last lived before being sent to prison; "resides" must be interpreted to mean a person's legal residence or domicile at the time of his incarceration.

Cashel v Regents of the University of Michigan, 141 Mich App 541; 367 NW2d 841 (1985)

Where a person seeking to inspect records will take more than two weeks to complete inspection, she may be assessed labor costs incurred by public body to supervise her inspection.

Soave v Michigan Department of Education, 139 Mich App 99; 360 NW2d 194 (1984)

Because federal agency regulations have the force and effect of federal statutory law, a state agency may properly withhold a record under FOIA, 13(1)(d) if that record is exempt from disclosure under a federal agency regulation.

Capitol Information Association v Ann Arbor Police Department, 138 Mich App 655; 360 NW2d 262 (1984)

Plaintiff's request, seeking "all correspondence" between local police department and "all federal law enforcement/investigative" agencies, was "absurdly overboard" and failed to sufficiently identify specific records as required by FOIA, 3(1).

Hoffman v Bay City School District, 137 Mich App 333; 357 NW2d 686 (1984)

Where an attorney conducted an investigation into the business and finance practices of a school district and orally reported his opinion regarding the investigation to the school board but did not share the actual documents, the investigative file itself is not a public record of the board.

Michigan State Employees Association v Department of Management and Budget, 135 Mich App 248; 353 NW2d 496 (1984)

The disclosure to a union of a list of the names and home addresses of public employees is not a clearly unwarranted invasion of the employees' privacy; such lists are, therefore, not exempt under FOIA, 13(1)(a).

Mullin v Detroit Police Department, 133 Mich App 46; 348 NW2d 708 (1984)

Defendant properly exempted a computer tape containing personal information on persons involved in traffic accidents. Disclosure of the tape would have been a clearly unwarranted invasion of privacy.

Evening News Association v City of Troy; 417 Mich 481; 339 NW2d 421 (1983)

A general claim that records are involved in an ongoing criminal investigation and that their disclosure would "interfere with law enforcement proceedings" is not sufficient to sustain an exemption under FOIA, § 13 (1)(b). A public body must indicate factually and in detail how a particular document or category of documents satisfies the exemption; mere conclusory allegations are not sufficient.

Dawkins v Department of Civil Service, 130 Mich App 669; 344 NW2d 43 (1983)

If a plaintiff in a FOIA case prevails only in part, she may be awarded either all of her court costs and attorney fees or only that portion fairly allocable to the successful portion of her case. The fact that the defendant's refusal to disclose the records was made in good faith and was not arbitrary or capricious has no bearing whatever on the plaintiff's right to recover these costs.

Bechtel Power Corp v Department of Treasury, 128 Mich App 324; 340 NW2d 297 (1983)

Tax information may be protected against disclosure under 13 (1) (a) and 13(1)(d) of FOIA.

Pennington v Washtenaw County Sheriff, 125 Mich App 556; 336 NW2d 828 (1983)

Failure to respond to a request is treated as a final decision to deny the request. A plaintiff need only make a showing in circuit court that the request was made and denied. The burden is on the defendant to show a viable defense. Non-disclosure based upon the privacy exemption of 13(1)(b)(iii) is limited to intimate details of a highly personal nature.

Perlongo v Iron River TV, 122 Mich App 433; 332 NW2d 502 (1983)

A private non stock, nonprofit cable television corporation is not a "public body" for purposes of either the Open meetings Act or the Freedom of Information Act, even though it is licensed, franchised, or otherwise regulated by the government.

Tobin v Michigan Civil Service Commission, 416 Mich 661; 331 NW2d 184 (1982)

The FOIA does not compel a public body to conceal information at the insistence of one who opposes its release.

Kestenbaum v Michigan State University, 414 Mich 510; 327 NW2d 783 (1982)

An equally divided supreme Court affirmed the lower court in holding that a list of names and addresses of students on a computer tape would appear to be a public record, but the nature of the information is personal and falls within an enumerated exception. Public disclosure of the tape would constitute a clearly unwarranted invasion of a person's privacy.

Ballard v Department of Corrections, 122 Mich App 123; 332 NW2d 435 (1982)

A film made by the Department of Corrections showing a prisoner being forcibly removed from his prison cell is a public record and must be disclosed. Exemption asserted by the DOC did not outweigh the public interest in disclosure.

International Union, UPGWA v Department of State Police, 118 Mich App 292; 324 NW2d 611 (1982), aff'd by equally divided court, 422 Mich 432 (1985)

The exemption of a list of names and home addresses of private security guards from disclosure to a union seeking that list for collective bargaining purposes is not justified. The public purpose of collective bargaining outweighs the employees' interest in the privacy of this information. However, the union is ordered not to engage in further disclosure of the list for other unrelated purposes.

Cashel v Smith, 117 Mich App 405; 324 NW2d 336 (1982)

Depositions may sometimes be appropriate in FOIA cases, but they must be justified. The Legislature intended that the flow of information from public bodies and persons should not be impeded by long court process.

Palladium Publishing Co v River Valley School District, 115 Mich App 490; 321 NW2d 705 (1982)

The name of student suspended by the action of a board of education will appear in the meeting minutes and is not information exempt from disclosure under the FOIA.

Ridenour v Dearborn Board of Education, 111 Mich App 798; 314 NW2d 760 (1981)

Public disclosure of performance evaluation of school administrators is not an intrusion of privacy as defined by FOIA because people have a strong interest in public education and because taxpayers are increasingly holding administrators accountable for expenditures of tax money.

Local 79, Service Employees International Union, AFL-CIO, Hospital Employees Division v Lapeer County General Hospital, 111 Mich App 441; 314 NW2d 648 (1981)

The proper forum in which to seek relief from a violation of the FOIA is the circuit court and not the Michigan Employment Relations Commission, notwithstanding labor-related issues.

Schinzel v Wilkerson, 110 Mich App 600; 313 NW2d 167 (1981)

A plaintiff appearing in propria persona who prevails in an action commenced pursuant to the Freedom of Information Act is entitled to an award of his actual expenditures, but is not entitled to an award of attorney fees.

Blue Cross/Blue Shield v Insurance Bureau, 104 Mich App 113; 304 NW2d 499 (1981)

Information may be revealed under FOIA despite claim of exemption. A decision to deny disclosure of exempt records is committed to discretion of agency and should not be disturbed unless abuse of discretion is found. Trade secret exemption does not apply to information required by law or as a condition of receiving a government contract, license or benefit.

Jordan v Martimucci, 101 Mich App 212; 300 NW2d 325 (1980)

A plaintiff who brings an action under the FOIA for punitive damages for delay in disclosure of requested information must demonstrate that he has received the requested information as a result of a court-ordered disclosure and that the defendant acted arbitrarily and capriciously in failing to comply with the disclosure request in a timely manner.

Nabkey v Kent Community Action Program, Inc., 99 Mich App 480; 298 NW2d 11 (1980).

No award of attorney fees is possible where a prevailing plaintiff under the FOIA is not represented by an attorney.

Bredemeier v Kentwood Board of Education, 95 Mich App 767; 291 NW2d 199 (1980)

The FOIA does not require that information be recorded by a public body, but if it is, it must be disclosed. Attorney fees, costs and disbursements are awarded to prevailing party under FOIA.

However, to prevail, a party must show at a minimum that bringing a court action was necessary and had a causative effect on delivery of the information. Lack of court-ordered disclosure precludes an award of punitive damages under FOIA.

Penokie v Michigan Technological University, 93 Mich App 650; 287 NW2d 304 (1979)

Disclosure of the names and salaries of employees of the defendant university is not a "clearly unwarranted" invasion of personal privacy under FOIA.

Booth Newspapers, Inc v Regents of University of Michigan, 93 Mich App 100; 286 NW2d 55 (1979)

The written opinion of a public body's attorney is exempt from disclosure under FOIA and may serve as a basis for closing a meeting under the OMA.

Williams v Martimucci, 88 Mich App 198; 276 NW2d 876 (1979)

Action of the manager of general office services at a state prison in denying inmate's request for copies of certain documents in inmate's file because inmate did not pay the $3 fee for the cost of processing the request was not arbitrary and capricious, since the manager checked the institutional indigency list for the month and found that the inmate's name was not on it.

Alpena Title, Inc v Alpena County, 84 Mich App 308; 269 NW2d 578 (1978)

A county board of commissioners may charge a reasonable fee for access to and the copying of county tract index information in accordance with the statute regarding fees for the inspection of such records.

Appendix 12

Freedom of Information Act

(For complete text see: http://www.ag.state.mi.us/)

MCL 15.243 Exemptions from disclosure; withholding of information required by law or in possession of executive office.

Sec. 13. (1) A public body may exempt from disclosure as a public record under this act:

(a) Information of a personal nature where the public disclosure of the information would constitute a clearly unwarranted invasion of an individual's privacy.

(b) Investigating records compiled for law enforcement purposes, but only to the extent that disclosure as a public record would do any of the following:

(i) Interfere with law enforcement proceedings.

(ii) Deprive a person of the right to a fair trial or impartial administrative adjudication.

(iii) Constitute an unwarranted invasion of personal privacy.

(iv) Disclose the identity of a confidential source, or if the record is compiled by a law enforcement agency in the course of a criminal investigation, disclose confidential information furnished only by a confidential source.

(v) Disclose law enforcement investigative techniques or procedures.

(vi) Endanger the life or physical safety of law enforcement personnel.

(c) A public record that if disclosed would prejudice a public body's ability to maintain the physical security of custodial or penal institutions occupied by persons arrested or convicted of a crime or admitted because of a mental disability, unless the public interest in disclosure under this act outweighs the public interest in nondisclosure.

(d) Records or information specifically described and exempted from disclosure by statute.

(e) Information the release of which would prevent the public body from complying with section 444 of subpart 4 of part C of the general education provisions act, title IV of Public Law 90-247, 20 U.S.C. 1232g, commonly referred to as the family educational rights and privacy act of 1974.

(f) A public record or information described in this section that is furnished by the public body originally compiling, preparing, or receiving the record or information to a public officer or public body in connection with the performance of the duties of that public officer or public body, if the considerations originally giving rise to the exempt nature of the public record remain applicable.

(g) Trade secrets or commercial or financial information voluntarily provided to an agency for use in developing governmental policy if:

(i) The information is submitted upon a promise of confidentiality by the public body.

(ii) The promise of confidentiality is authorized by the chief administrative officer of the public body or by an elected official at the time the promise is made.

(iii) A description of the information is recorded by the public body within a reasonable time after it has been submitted, maintained in a central place within the public body, and made available to a person upon request. This subdivision does not apply to information submitted as required by law or as a condition of receiving a governmental contract, license, or other benefit.

(h) Information or records subject to the attorney-client privilege.

(i) Information or records subject to the physician-patient privilege, the psychologist-patient privilege, the minister, priest, or Christian Science practitioner privilege, or other privilege recognized by statute or court rule.

(j) A bid or proposal by a person to enter into a contract or agreement, until the time for the public opening of bids or proposals, or if a public opening is not to be conducted, until the deadline for submission of bids or proposals has expired.

(k) Appraisals of real property to be acquired by the public body until (i) an agreement is entered into; or (ii) 3 years has elapsed since the making of the appraisal, unless litigation relative to the acquisition has not yet terminated.

(l) Test questions and answers, scoring keys, and other examination instruments or data used to administer a license, public employment, or academic examination, unless the public interest in disclosure under this act outweighs the public interest in nondisclosure.

(m) Medical, counseling, or psychological facts or evaluations concerning an individual if the individual's identity would be revealed by a disclosure of those facts or evaluation.

(n) Communications and notes within a public body or between public bodies of an advisory nature to the extent that they cover other than purely factual materials and are preliminary to a final agency determination of policy or action. This exemption does not apply unless the public body shows that in the particular instance the public interest in encouraging frank communications between officials and employees of public bodies clearly outweighs the public interest in disclosure. This exemption does not constitute an exemption under state law for purposes of section 8(h) of the open meetings act, Act No. 267 of the Public Acts of 1976, being section 15.268 of the Michigan Compiled Laws. As used in this subdivision, "determination of policy or action" includes a determination relating to collective bargaining, unless the public record is otherwise required to be made available under Act No. 336 of the Public Acts of 1947, being sections 423.201 to 423.217 of the Michigan Compiled Laws.

(o) Records of law enforcement communication codes, or plans for deployment of law enforcement personnel, that if disclosed would prejudice a public body's ability to protect the public safety unless the public interest in disclosure under this act weighs the public interest in nondisclosure in the particular instance.

(p) Information that would reveal the exact location of archaeological sites. The secretary of state may promulgate rules pursuant to the administrative procedures act of 1969, Act No. 306 of the Public Acts of 1969, being sections 24.201 to 24.328 of the Michigan Compiled Laws, to provide for the disclosure of the location of archaeological sites for purposes relating to the preservation or scientific examination of sites.

(q) Testing data developed by a public body in determining whether bidders' products meet the specifications for purchase of those products by the public body, if disclosure of the data would reveal that only 1 bidder has met the specifications. This subdivision does not apply after 1 year has elapsed from the time the public body completes the testing.

(r) Academic transcripts of an institution of higher education established under section 5, 6, or 7 of article VIII of the state constitution of 1963, if the transcript pertains to a student who is delinquent in the payment of financial obligations to the institution.

(s) Records of any campaign committee including any committee that receives money from a state campaign fund.

(t) Unless the public interest in disclosure outweighs the public interest in nondisclosure in the particular instance, public records of a law enforcement agency, the release of which would do any of the following:

(i) Identify or provide a means of identifying an informer.

(ii) Identify or provide a means of identifying a law enforcement undercover officer or agent or a plain clothes officer as a law enforcement officer or agent.

(iii) Disclose the personal address or telephone number of law enforcement officers or agents or any special skills that they may have.

(iv) Disclose the name, address, or telephone numbers of family members, relatives, children, or parents of law enforcement officers or agents.

(v) Disclose operational instructions for law enforcement officers or agents.

(vi) Reveal the contents of staff manuals provided for law enforcement officers or agents.

(vii) Endanger the life or safety of law enforcement officers or agents or their families, relatives, children, parents, or those who furnish information to law enforcement departments or agencies.

(viii) Identify or provide a means of identifying a person as a law enforcement officer, agent, or informer.

(ix) Disclose personnel records of law enforcement agencies.

(x) Identify or provide a means of identifying residences that law enforcement agencies are requested to check in the absence of their owners or tenants.

(u) Except as otherwise provided in this subdivision, records and information pertaining to an investigation or a compliance conference conducted by the department of consumer and industry services under article 15 of the public health code, Act No. 368 of the Public Acts of 1978, being sections 333.16101 to 333.18838 of the Michigan Compiled Laws, before a complaint is issued. This subdivision does not apply to records and information pertaining to 1 or more of the following:

(i) The fact that an allegation has been received and an investigation is being conducted, and the date the allegation was received.

(ii) The fact that an allegation was received by the department of consumer and industry services; the fact that the department of consumer and industry services did not issue a complaint for the allegation; and the fact that the allegation was dismissed.

(v) Records of a public body's security measures, including security plans, security codes and combinations, passwords, passes, keys, and security procedures, to the extent that the records relate to the ongoing security of the public body.

(w) Records or information relating to a civil action in which the requesting party and the public body are parties.

(x) Information or records that would disclose the social security number of any individual.

(y) Except as otherwise provided in this subdivision, an application for the position of president of an institution of higher education established under section 4, 5, or 6 of article VIII of the state constitution of 1963, materials submitted with such an application, letters of recommendation or references concerning an applicant, and records or information relating to the process of searching for and selecting an individual for a position described in this subdivision, if the records or information could be used to identify a candidate for the position. However, after 1 or more individuals have been identified as finalists for a position described in this subdivision, this subdivision does not apply to a public record described in this subdivision, except a letter of recommendation or reference, to the extent that the public record relates to an individual identified as a finalist for the position.

(2) This act does not authorize the withholding of information otherwise required by law to be made available to the public or to a party in a contested case under Act No. 306 of the Public Acts of 1969.

(3) Except as otherwise exempt under subsection (1) , this act does not authorize the withholding of a public record in the possession of the executive office of the governor or lieutenant governor, or an employee of either executive office, if the public record is transferred to the executive office of the governor or lieutenant governor, or an employee of either executive office, after a request for the public record has been received by a state officer, employee, agency, department, division, bureau, board, commission, council, authority, or other body in the executive branch of government that is subject to this act.

History: 1976, Act 442, Eff. Apr. 13, 1977;--Am. 1978, Act 329, Imd. Eff. July 11, 1978;--Am. 1993, Act 82, Eff. Apr. 1, 1994;--Am. 1996, Act 553, Eff. Mar. 31, 1997.

BIBLIOGRAPHY FOR REPORTER'S GUIDE TO MICHIGAN MEDIA LAW

"Your Right to Privacy; a Basic Guide to Legal Rights in an Information Society," the American Civil Liberties Union, Dept. L. PO Box 794, Medford, N.Y. 11763. $9.45. U.S. Freedom of Information Act users guide, 1755 Massachusetts Ave. N.W, Suite 500, Washington, D.C. 20036.

Information on U.S. FOIA – 1(202) 514-3642

Michigan FOIA 1 - (313) 577-8379.

"Libel Law and the Press, by Randall P. Bezansons, Gilbert Cranberg and John Soloski, The Free Press, a division of Macmillan Inc. 1987, New York.

Florida Media Law, 2nd edition) by Donna Lee Dickerson, University of South Florida Press, 1991, Tampa.

The First Amendment and the Fourth Estate, The Law of Mass Media (6th edition), by T. Barton Carter, Marc A. Franklin, and Jay B. Wright., The Foundation Press, Inc., 1994, Westbury, N.Y,

"Case History, The Protection of Times V. Sullivan freed the press from the whims of aggrieved public figures," by Anthony Lewis, News Inc. Magazine, April 1992 pps. 26-30.

"Case Study, Sullivan opened the door to troublesome meddling into how journalists do their jobs, " by Randall Bezanson, News Inc. Magazine, April 1992, pps. 30-31.

Michigan's Freedom of Information Act and Open Meetings Act, Prepared by State Rep. Lyn R. Bankes, Livonia, 1990.

Legal Guidelines for Reporters in Michigan, Revised and Updated, by Jane Briggs-Bunting, PO Box 7, Oxford, MI 48371, 1993.

Tapping Officials" Secrets, The Door to Open Government in Michigan, Reporters Committee for Freedom of the Press, PO Box 33756, Washington, D.,C. 20033, 1989.

Mass Communications Law in North Carolina, by Ruth Walden, New Forums Press Inc. Stillwater, Okla. 1993

Mass Communication Law in Virginia, by W. Wat Hopkins, endorsed by the Virginia Press Association, New Forums Press, Stillwater, OKLA. 1993.

Index

Chapter & Page

Chapter & Page

Chapter & Page

Chapter & Page

Chapter & Page

Cases: **Chapter & Page**

Cases: **Chapter & Page**

Cases: **Chapter & Page**